First World War
and Army of Occupation
War Diary
France, Belgium and Germany

3 DIVISION
Divisional Troops
5(A) Sanitary Section
14 January 1916 - 31 March 1917

WO95/1408/2

Published by

The Naval & Military Press Ltd

Unit 10 Ridgewood Industrial Park,

Uckfield, East Sussex,

TN22 5QE England

Tel: +44 (0) 1825 749494

www.naval-military-press.com

www.nmarchive.com

This diary has been reprinted in facsimile from the original. Any imperfections are inevitably reproduced and the quality may fall short of modern type and cartographic standards.

© **Crown Copyright**
Images reproduced by permission of The National Archives, London, England, 2015.

Contents

Document type	Place/Title	Date From	Date To
Heading	WO95/1408/2		
Heading	3rd Division Medical 5A Sanitary Section 1916 1917 March 1 Army April 17		
Heading	3rd War Diary of O.C 5A Sanitary Section III Division From Jan 17, 1916 To Feb 29. 1916 Vol I		
War Diary	Field	14/01/1916	23/01/1916
War Diary	Reninghelst	24/01/1916	07/02/1916
War Diary	Field	08/02/1916	08/02/1916
War Diary	Nordausques	09/02/1916	29/02/1916
Heading	3rd 5A Sany Section March 1916		
Heading	5 Sanitary Sec Vol II		
War Diary	Nordausques	01/03/1916	06/03/1916
War Diary	Field	07/03/1916	07/03/1916
War Diary	Reninghelst	08/03/1916	31/03/1916
Heading	War Diary of No. 5a Sanitary Section 3rd Division For April 1916		
Miscellaneous		04/05/1916	04/05/1916
War Diary	Reninghelst	01/04/1916	06/04/1916
War Diary	Meteren	07/04/1916	26/04/1916
War Diary	Westoutre	27/04/1916	30/04/1916
Heading	No 5a Sanitary Section May 1916		
War Diary	Westoutre	01/05/1916	27/05/1916
War Diary	Meteren	28/05/1916	31/05/1916
Heading	Vol 5 War Diary of oc 5a Sanitary Section 3rd Division June 1916		
War Diary	Meteren	01/06/1916	14/06/1916
War Diary	Field	18/06/1916	20/06/1916
War Diary	Tilques	21/06/1916	30/06/1916
Heading	3rd Division 5a Sanitary Section July 1916		
War Diary	Tilques	01/07/1916	01/07/1916
War Diary	Field	02/07/1916	10/07/1916
War Diary	Carnoy	11/07/1916	12/07/1916
War Diary	Montauban	13/07/1916	16/07/1916
War Diary	Bronfay Farm	17/07/1916	26/07/1916
War Diary	Field	27/07/1916	27/07/1916
War Diary	Treux	28/07/1916	28/07/1916
War Diary	Ville	29/07/1916	31/07/1916
Heading	Vol 7 War Diary of O.C. 5A Sanitary Section 3rd Division For The Month Of August 1916		
War Diary	Ville sur Ancre	01/08/1916	01/08/1916
War Diary	Ville	02/08/1916	15/08/1916
War Diary	Little Bear Copse	16/08/1916	19/08/1916
War Diary	Meaulte	20/08/1916	22/08/1916
War Diary	Field	23/08/1916	23/08/1916
War Diary	Bernaville	24/08/1916	24/08/1916
War Diary	Field	25/08/1916	26/08/1916
War Diary	Nouex-Les-Mines	27/08/1916	27/08/1916
War Diary	Nouex	28/08/1916	31/08/1916
Heading	3rd Division No 5a Sanitary Section Sept 1916		

Heading	Vol 8 War Diary of O.C 5A Sanitary Section 3rd Division		
War Diary	Novex-Les-Mines	01/09/1916	08/09/1916
War Diary	Novex	09/09/1916	22/09/1916
War Diary	Field	23/09/1916	24/09/1916
War Diary	Bomy	25/09/1916	30/09/1916
War Diary	140/1488 3rd Division 5a Sanitary Section Oct 1916		
Heading	Vol 9 War Diary of O.C 5A Sanitary Section For October 1916		
War Diary	Bomy	01/10/1916	04/10/1916
War Diary	Field	05/10/1916	07/10/1916
War Diary	Bertrancourt	08/10/1916	17/10/1916
War Diary	Field	18/10/1916	18/10/1916
War Diary	Bus-Les-Artois	19/10/1916	31/10/1916
Heading	140/1846 Vol 10 3rd Div War Diary of O.C 5A Sanitary Section 3rd division For November 1916		
War Diary	Bus	01/11/1916	30/11/1916
Heading	140/1900 Vol XI 3rd Div War Diary of 5a Sanitary Section From 1 Dec 16 To 31 Dec 16		
War Diary	Bus	01/12/1916	31/12/1916
Heading	140/1941 Vol 12 3rd Division War Diary of OC 5a Sanitary Section January 1917		
War Diary	Bus	01/01/1917	28/01/1917
War Diary	Field	29/01/1917	30/01/1917
War Diary	Villers Chatel	31/01/1917	31/01/1917
Heading	140/1994 Medical Vol 13 3rd Div War Diary of O.C 5A Sanitary Section For February 1917		
War Diary	Villers Chatel	01/02/1917	08/02/1917
War Diary	Lignereuil	09/02/1917	11/02/1917
War Diary	Wanquetin	12/02/1917	28/02/1917
Heading	140/2043 3rd Division (S) No 5a Sanitary Section March 1917		
War Diary	Vol 14 War Diary of O.C 5a Sanitary Section For March 1917		
War Diary	Warlus	01/03/1917	31/03/1917

washing(2)
wash/non8(2)

3RD DIVISION
MEDICAL

5A SANITARY SECTION
1916 JAN ~~DEC 1916~~. 1917 MARCH

I. 1ST ARMY APRIL 17

To: Office
c/c A.G's. Office
at the Base.

CONFIDENTIAL

WAR DIARY OF.

O.C. 5A SANITARY SECTION
III. DIVISION

FROM JAN. 17. 1916 to FEB. 29. 1916.

Vol I

E.L.Matthews
Lt RAMC
O.C. San Sec.
III. Div.

WAR DIARY
or
INTELLIGENCE SUMMARY.
(Erase heading not required.)

Army Form C. 2118

Hour, Date, Place	Summary of Events and Information	Remarks and references to Appendices
19.1.16. Field.	Forenoon visited Camps E, B&C, 4th Ordon. Found following matters needed attention. **Camp E.** (1) Covered receptacle needed at incinerator for faeces. (2) New urine pit required. **Camp 4th Ordon.** New urine pit required at latrine. Softening medium regd for shower & ablution bench. **Camps B&C** New screening & cover required for latrine tubs. Back shields needed for urine tubs. No covered receptacle for faeces. Softening medium required for grease trap & ablution bench drainage. **Afternoon.** Office routine. (laundry, bath & sanitary) Visit from H/Sgr Peacock 151 NZIA — discussion re prevention of lice. 11 pm. Inspected drying sheds stables, found all in order.	

WAR DIARY
or
INTELLIGENCE SUMMARY.
(Erase heading not required.)

Army Form C. 2118

Hour, Date, Place	Summary of Events and Information	Remarks and references to Appendices
18.1.16.	**Forenoon** Investigated complaints re dirty clothing at baths & condition of latrine. Gave further instruction re scrubbing of clothing. Decided to shift latrine to new site as soon as labour available. Inspected H.Q. Offices & found latrine in every case in an unsatisfactory condition requiring new screening, roofs & generally cleaning up. Reorganised sanitary squads in H.Q. the 4 numbers numbered to 1 NCO. + 3 men. Gave instructions for work to be carried out at Guedelle & Louville. **Afternoon.** Office routine, new drying sheds. 11.15 p.m. Inspected drying sheds & found all in order.	
19.1.16.	**Forenoon.** To 2nd Suffolk & R.W.F. camp near DICKEBUSCH. Battalion moving from tents into huts. Urine trough fitted to latrine peak plates to be satisfactory, no straining material for waste ablution water. Found certain amount of general rubbish + tins in R.W.F. transport lines, also a man [out?] in to clean up. **Afternoon.** Inspected various sites in RENINGHELST. Great accumulation of horse manure at back of C.R.A. Office. Latrine buckets reqd. in 3rd Div. Signallers Transport lines. Orders known publish	

Army Form C. 2118.

WAR DIARY
or
INTELLIGENCE SUMMARY.
(Erase heading not required.)

Instructions regarding War Diaries and Intelligence Summaries are contained in F. S. Regs., Part II and the Staff Manual respectively. Title pages will be prepared in manuscript.

Hour, Date, Place	Summary of Events and Information	Remarks and references to Appendices
19.1.16. Field.	An old incinerator to be buried. Found new latrine being erected at saw mills. At R.E. Dump, RENING HELST, found new latrine satisfactory. Brick memorials being erected. Hedge to W. of G Office again fouled with faeces. Thralis chambers examined by S/sgt Mech. Transport & found satisfactory condition. Office routine.	
20.1.16. Field.	A.M. Inspected sites. Found all correct. A/16 K.R.R. Rongate advanced A.H.Q. (WOODCOTE HOUSE). Inspected new dug out. Complaint was made of has smell when dug out. Found that dug out has been built near a cesspool which was broken into during the building & part of the earth covering the cesspool had been put in sandbags & placed in dug out. General sanitary arrangements of H.Q. is satisfactory & failure will allow. 10.30 pm. Inspected drying sheds. Found all correct.	
21.1.16. Field.	Forenoon. Visited 1.R.B. Comp. Fires at present being burned but will be burnt as soon as brick can be drawn for an incinerator. As the ground under wire buckets is becoming very bad with him, suggested that dipping wire brick sheds be provided there were no grease traps at cookhouse & inadequate drainage.	

Army Form C. 2118.

WAR DIARY
or
INTELLIGENCE SUMMARY.
(Erase heading not required.)

Instructions regarding War Diaries and Intelligence Summaries are contained in F.S. Regs., Part II. and the Staff Manual respectively. Title pages will be prepared in manuscript.

Hour, Date, Place	Summary of Events and Information	Remarks and references to Appendices
	arrangement of ablution bench. Visited L.R.B. transport lines. Suggested that roof be provided for their latrine. Grease trap being filled up at cookhouse. Visited North'd Fusiliers transport lines. Drainage ditches required at ablution bench, + roof for latrine. Duckboards being laid down. Dealt with strike of washerwomen employed in connection with laundry. Afternoon. Office routine + various matters connected with bath, laundry + drying shed. Arranged for drainage of camp site at Div. bath. 11.15 p.m. Inspected drying sheds + found everything satisfactory.	
22.1.16. Field.	Visited reservoirs at foot of MONT ROUGE supplying water to stand pipe on WESTOUTRE road. Afternoon. Visited transport lines of 13th Kings (Liverpool) Regt + 4th Royal Fusiliers. Camps are in very muddy condition but work is still being done in them, + a system of paths w duck walks will be provided meanie taken away.	

Army Form C. 2118.

WAR DIARY
or
INTELLIGENCE SUMMARY.
(Erase heading not required.)

Instructions regarding War Diaries and Intelligence Summaries are contained in F.S. Regs., Part II. and the Staff Manual respectively. Title pages will be prepared in manuscript.

Hour, Date, Place	Summary of Events and Information	Remarks and references to Appendices
23.1.16 Feb	Daily by farmer. Visited YYLSLI transport lines, found them in satisfactory condition. 10.45 am. Inspected drying sheds, found all correct. Court of Enquiry at Div. HQrs. RENINGHELST to enquire into loss of clothing during fire on Jan 13. Drew 5560 francs on imprest account. Paid women employed by laundry. Afternoon. Paid section men + attached regimental fatigue men. Office routine. 11 am. Inspected drying sheds, found all in order. Repairing of two stoves in No 1 shed requires slight repairs.	

WAR DIARY of O.C. SA Sanitary Section Army Form C. 2118
or
INTELLIGENCE SUMMARY
III Division

(Erase heading not required.)

Instructions regarding War Diaries and Intelligence Summaries are contained in F.S. Regs., Part II and the Staff Manual respectively. Title pages will be prepared in manuscript.

Hour, Date, Place	Summary of Events and Information	Remarks and references to Appendices
24.1.16. RENINGHELST.	Forenoon. Stock taking of socks. Total rendered to Q Office. Inspected D camp (M.S.L.I.) + found that recommendations made in former inspection are being carried out viz: ① Ablution benches are being enlarged + properly drained + will eventually be covered in ② New grease traps have been constructed + are reported to be satisfactory ③ Latrines are being covered in. New latrine has been built. Afternoon. Office routine. Arranging lecture on methods of meeting gas attacks. 11 p.m. Inspected drying huts found all in order.	
25.1.16. RENINGHELST.	Forenoon. To 8 E. Yorks Transport lines. These lines are in an exceedingly muddy condition. A quantity of turf + general rubbish was lying about. Latrine arrangements were very unsatisfactory + consisted of two empty creosote tins filled to the brim with faeces.	

WAR DIARY of O.C. 5A Sanitary Section
III Division
INTELLIGENCE SUMMARY

Army Form C 2118.

Place	Date	Hour	Summary of Events and Information	Remarks and references to Appendices
RENINGHELST 2/4.	25/1/16		Attention of Transport sergeant + Regt Q.M. was drawn to unsatisfactory condition of Transport lines. I was informed that transport is shortly moving to new site. (Sy Inf Bde). Inspected "I" camp. Items following defect needing attention: ① Owing to latrine buckets being constantly replaced after emptying some men had been urinating on the ground + missing the bucket with the result that a stream of urine was flowing out at back of latrine + ground inside latrine was foul. As buckets were numbered shallow instructions were given that they were to be raised from the ground + more care exercised in replacing them after emptying. ② The ground inside the Officers latrine has become rather foul + a considerable quantity of paper was lying about. As the latrine was small it was suggested that it should be moved to fresh site. ③ Bricks were secured by Sanitary N.C.O. for manufacture of a strainer at the ablution benches. This has not yet been done the drains from the ablution bench also require cleaning out. A drainage pit from manure heaps in a farm at the entrance to the camp was causing considerable offence at the time of visit. It was suggested that this should	

Army Form C. 2118.

Instructions regarding War Diaries and Intelligence Summaries are contained in F. S. Regs., Part II. and the Staff Manual respectively. Title pages will be prepared in manuscript.

WAR DIARY of O.C. Sanitary Section III Division
or
INTELLIGENCE SUMMARY.
(Erase heading not required.)

Place	Date	Hour	Summary of Events and Information	Remarks and references to Appendices
RENINGHELST 25.1.16			Be cleaned out as soon as possible. Although apparently it is undoubtedly a menace to the health of the troops occupying the camp in the vicinity of the cesspool. Afternoon. Office routine. 11mm suspects drying shed found all in order.	
Do.	26.1.16	Forenoon. To 42nd Brigade batteries. A.C.		
		45th Battery.	Faeces are being buried in open incinerators well away from the camp. No offence is noticeable. Urine is boiled then spread on the land. Boundary ditch of camp was stifled up & overflowing. Instructions were given that same should be cleared.	
		41st Battery.	Incinerators require rebuilding. Latrine appears to be gradually falling forward & supports require re-erection.	
		Bde H.Q.	Incinerators require rebuilding. Traces in both cases being burned on the incinerator.	
		Afternoon. 29th R. Battery.	(1) Men were found to be missing the bucket urinating on the ground. Instructions were given that buckets should be raised. (2) Found that straw in barns occupied by men was only changed	

WAR DIARY or INTELLIGENCE SUMMARY

Army Form C. 2118.

O.C. 5th Sanitary Sec.
III Division

Place	Date	Hour	Summary of Events and Information	Remarks and references to Appendices
RENINGHELST	26.1.16		Once a week as camp was very muddy it was suggested that straw should be changed as often as possible. S.M. states that straw wisps be changed every other day. Faeces are being burned on their incinerator well away from the camp. No offence is noticeable. Inspected drying sheds, found all in order. 10.30 p.m.	
do	27.1.16		Forenoon. Inspected various H.Q. offices in RENINGHELST. I found that various defects noted in last him have been or are being remedied. Latrine seat has been enlarged, fly's bucket provided. Urine bucket has been also placed in latrine. Officers Club. G. office has received two provided for latrines. Incinerator has been cleared up incinerator is to be rebuilt as soon as labour is available. Latrine seat requires permitting. Burris Quarters of two still lying about - latrine required new fittings which details in afternoon in attempt to his & also to M.P. billet which require draining & cleaning up.	

WAR DIARY of O.E. SA Sanitary Sec
                III Division

or

INTELLIGENCE SUMMARY.

Army Form C. 2118.

(Erase heading not required.)

Instructions regarding War Diaries and Intelligence
Summaries are contained in F. S. Regs., Part II.
and the Staff Manual respectively. Title pages
will be prepared in manuscript.

Place	Date	Hour	Summary of Events and Information	Remarks and references to Appendices
RENINGHELST	27.1.16	Afternoon	Inspected piles of old F & G camps found quantity of tins & general rubbish still lying about. As soon as gun boots can be obtained these sites will be cleared. New incinerator has been erected at R.E. dump & appears to be satisfactory. Office routine. 11 pm. Inspected drying shed. Found all in order	
do	28.1.16	Forenoon	Inspected various R.E. units. 192nd Coy has ablution bench being erected. Advised as to draining for bench also as to burning of faeces construction of grease trap. 1st E Riding Fd Cy. Grease trap unsatisfactory, leading into open pit. Faeces are not being burned. Ablution tub Cy. New incinerator being erected. Grease trap requires cleaning out. Additional straining material also required. Site of do requires cleaning up.	

1577 Wt. W10791/1773 500,000 1/15 D. D. & L. A.D.S.S./Forms/C. 2118.

WAR DIARY of O.C. 57 Sanitary Sec., III Division   Army Form C.2118.

or

~~INTELLIGENCE SUMMARY.~~

(Erase heading not required.)

Place	Date	Hour	Summary of Events and Information	Remarks and references to Appendices
RENINGHELST	28.1.16		Cheshire Fees Co. (contd). A few empty crear tins are being used in the latrine + do not appear to be very satisfactory. It is also however that at present latrine buckets cannot be obtained.	
			Afternoon: General work in connection with drainage improvement of camp site + enlargement of trails with a view to preventing lice.	
			= 1 p.m. Inspected drying sheds. Found all in order.	
do	29.1.16	Forenoon	To J camp (12 W. Yorks), also detail + transport camps of R.Scots + W. Yorks. Urine scoop fitted to latrine at J camp requires repairing + reconstructing. An extra incinerator is needed to dispose of rubbish in J. transport camp run Yorks. The package pit of the ablution benches requires cleaning out.	
		Afternoon	Office routine	
		12 midnight	Inspected drying sheds. Found all in order.	
do	30.1.16		Drew 2000 francs in respect a/c Paid women employed by laundry.	
		Afternoon	Lecture on defensive measures against fly attack. Office routine h. 45. Drying sheds. Found all in order.	

WAR DIARY of O.C. 5A Sanitary Section III Division

INTELLIGENCE SUMMARY
(Erase heading not required.)

Army Form C. 2118.

Place	Date	Hour	Summary of Events and Information	Remarks and references to Appendices
RENINGHELST	31.1.16		Forenoon. Drew out plan for enlargement of baths & adoption of preventive measures against lice. Inspected Y.M.C.A. site & found a certain amount of public rubbish accumulated during building of new marquee. Gave instructions for it to be collected & burnt. Afternoon. Office routine. 11 hrs. Inspected drying sheds found all in order.	
do	1.2.16		Forenoon. To DICKEBUSCH. In main street of village long bottle of stagnant water have formed. Some of the ditches & cellars of ruined houses are also full of water. Saw middlar pit & two cesspits in houses occupied by 3rd Div. troops also require cleaning out. Saw M.A.D.S. on subject & will arrange for a vidange to be sent up as soon as possible. Afternoon. Office routine. Wrote plants on interior of Div. baths. Arranged for cleaning up of sundry sites in RENINGHELST vicinity. 12 midnight. Inspected drying sheds & found all in order.	

WAR DIARY

of O.C. 'A' Sanitary Section
II Division

Army Form C. 2118

INTELLIGENCE SUMMARY

(Erase heading not required.)

Place	Date	Hour	Summary of Events and Information	Remarks and references to Appendices
RENINGHELST	2.2.16		Forenoon. To camp of 4 K GORDONS. Recommendations made in last visit are being acted upon viz. (1) A trick incinerator has been built by burning refuse. Covers receptacle have been provided for feces. Some difficulty is experienced in obtaining sawdust. It was suggested that straw might be used or absorbent material might be obtained from neighbouring mill (chaff or milling refuse) (2) Urine trough has been moved to other end of latrine lines were put constructed. A few minor improvements were suggested (3) Shaving material has been provided at ablution benches. (4) The cookhouse is being shifted to a position further removed from the incinerator & latrine. New grease trap recently satisfactory. To 8 K Bde H.Q. A quantity of bones & lately tins has been deposited in a mud road near the camp. These were ordered up before he infection was fumed. Afternoon. Inspected old camp site found great quantity of tins & general rubbish, latrine pails, clothing etc lying about. Detailed squad to clean up.	

WAR DIARY or INTELLIGENCE SUMMARY.

Army Form C. 2118.

of A.D.M.S. 57 Sanitary Section
57 Division

Place	Date	Hour	Summary of Events and Information	Remarks and references to Appendices
RENINGHELST	2/1/16		Forenoon. To B. camp (K.O.R.L.) Recommendations made on last visit of inspection have been acted upon, viz:- ① Latrine has been covered in. Three buckets have been provided with flock covers. ② Covered receptacles have been provided at incinerator. The incinerator have been covered in (waterfall type). The roof of one shed was found to be too close to incinerator chimney. Attention of M.O. drawn to this. A small latrine for warrant officers only was found to be in an unduly condition. M.O. (his labelle appeared to the) was suggested to M.O. that it should be done away with. This was agreed to. Afternoon. To D camp (K.S.L.I.) Ablution benches have been enlarged & covered in. The screening from latrine has been torn away by the wind & suggestion was made to M.O. that the site of the latrine should be placed as the camp is in an exposed position.	

WAR DIARY
or
INTELLIGENCE SUMMARY

Army Form C. 2118.

O.C. 57 Sanitary Section 19th Division

Instructions regarding War Diaries and Intelligence Summaries are contained in F.S. Regs., Part II. and the Staff Manual respectively. Title pages will be prepared in manuscript.

Place	Date	Hour	Summary of Events and Information	Remarks and references to Appendices
RENINGHELST 3W6			The grease traps owing to unforeseen cause has been filled up & a separate butcher refuse was lying outside from fairly the shape. The cooks were Normanshy by two & men were detailed to clean out the grease trap & latch the refuse to the incinerator. A number of empty tins appeared to have been thrown on the hedge into the fields adjoining the camp. To L.R.B. camp. The Battalion has just moved out on very short notice but camp was fairly tidy but conditions. An N.C.O. has been left behind to complete clearing up of refuse & a corporal of the Sanitary Section was detailed to supervise & assist. Office routine. 11.30 To 23rd Bde R.A.V.S.	
do	4.2.16	Forenoon	Surfaced army sheep steps found all in order. Bde. H.Q. 4.A.C. were in very muddy condition but general sanitary arrangements appear to be satisfactory 104 R Bty. A brick incinerator is being built for disposing of faeces.	

WAR DIARY

of O.C. 5A Sanitary Section, III Division

(Erase heading not required.)

Place	Date	Hour	Summary of Events and Information	Remarks and references to Appendices
RENINGHELST	4.2.16		There was no grease trap at cookhouse and directions for construction were given to Q.M.S. One latrine requires no renewing. There were no urine buckets at latrines & it was suggested that empty cresol tins should be provided for the purpose. 108 I.R. Bty. Brick incinerator has been built for burning faeces. It was noted that an enclosed dump should be made for incinerator rubbish. Cookhouse refuse is fed to pigs. It was found that from cookhouse were being thrown night soil first latrine. Directions were given that they should be sent to incinerator. 109 L (Hy.) Empty tins are being used as urine in latrine. Latrine buckets O.M.S. was informed that required number of buckets would be supplied by Sanitary Section if transport could be provided by battery.

Afternoon: Office routine. Preparation for Div: move. Inspected sleeping quarters & found all in order.

10.30 hrs. | |

WAR DIARY
or
INTELLIGENCE SUMMARY.

Army Form C. 2118.

of O.C. 57 Sanitary Section
W. Dwain

Place	Date	Hour	Summary of Events and Information	Remarks and references to Appendices
RENNINGHELST	5.2.16		Forenoon. To horse lines of E.Yorks transport camp. Has not been cleaned up & is in satisfactory condition. "I" camp (8 E.Yorks). Inspected camp with the Battalion M.O. not yet moved in. but camp not in tidy condition. Cookhouse latrines & ablution benches has been cleaned up & rubbish deposits of incinerator was being disposed of quickly as possible. I camp. This camp has been left in satisfactory condition by 2 ROYAL SCOTS.	
		Afternoon	To D camp (KSLI). The camp was left in clean condition. Small latrine by medical hut requires emptying. Instructions were given to Sanitary Section men on incinerator to do so. To 4th GORDON camp. This camp was left in tidy & clean condition. Office routine. 1/8pm Inspected slits found all in order.	

1577 Wt. W10791/1773 500,000 1/15 D. D. & L. A.D.S.S./Forms/C. 2118.

WAR DIARY of O.C. 57A Sanitary Sec. III Division

INTELLIGENCE SUMMARY

Place	Date	Hour	Summary of Events and Information	Remarks and references to Appendices
RENINGHELST	6.2.16	Forenoon	To Camp of 1st GORDONS. Camp was left in fairly clean condition. Ground in vicinity however was rather foul but has been sprinkled with chloride of lime. Rubbish has been carelessly dumped at incinerator without that care which was shewn in arrangement with regard to latrines. Instructions were given to have disposal or incinerator of camp refuse be cleaned up. Paw womens gulleys by laundry. Drew 6000 francs in infantry a/c. To 4th Camp 10 R.W.K. This camp was left in rather an unsightly condition. Rubbish has been swept out of huts & left outside, not cleared away. This occupies by haversack men where very unlikely later. Old clothes, boots & lying about. Site & type of camp was inspected. This were lying about in rear & front of the camp & an old latrine site was found to be rather bad, bason lying in grouna pools of water, called attention of OVN & of Suffolk was called to this, +	

WAR DIARY
or
INTELLIGENCE SUMMARY

Army Form C. 2118.

H.Q.E. 5A Sanitary Section
T. Dewsnap

Place	Date	Hour	Summary of Events and Information	Remarks and references to Appendices
RENINGHELST	6.2.16		Instructions given that coal pits was to be cleaned up. O.C. MR Division arrived to take over. Afternoon — Paid men of section & attached regimental fatigue. Office routine. 10 p.m. Inspected drying sheds. Found all in order.	
do	7.2.16		To D camp (I.N. Fowlers) Camp was left in clean condition. A certain amount of kitchen refuse was found at back of cookhouse. The section man in the incinerator no details to clear this away. Stock taking of underclothes, appliances etc. Handing over to MR Division. 1 N.Co. 13 men details to clear up H.Qr. office wash site in RENINGHELST.	

WAR DIARY of O.C. 52 Sanitary Section III Division

INTELLIGENCE SUMMARY

Army Form C. 2118.

(Erase heading not required.)

Place	Date	Hour	Summary of Events and Information	Remarks and references to Appendices
Field	8.2.16		Section moved out from RENINGHELST; staff sergt. & men by rail to AUDRUICQ thence by road to NORDAUSQUES; lorry by road. Lorry broke down near CASSEL. Left lorry in charge Pte Co. & Jones 142 F.A. Wries to Div. F.A. Workshop unit.	
NORDAUSQUES	9.2.16		By road to HOULLE, thence to NORDAUSQUES.	
do	10.2.16		Arranges billets for men & orderly room for unit. Squads detailed to clear up billets in NORDAUSQUES. To CASSEL from that F.A.W.U. has been unable to locate lorry. Brought away stationery sundry equipment to F.A.W.U. Explains exact position of lorry. Inspects billets in NORDAUSQUES. Office routine.	
do	11.2.16			
do	12.2.16		1 NCO + 12 men detailed for sanitary duties at billets of 40th Bde RFA. Reports received from NCO's i/c men detailed for sanitary supervision with units.	

WAR DIARY or INTELLIGENCE SUMMARY.

Army Form C. 2118.

of A.D.S. 57 Sanitary Section
III Division

(Erase heading not required.)

Instructions regarding War Diaries and Intelligence Summaries are contained in F. S. Regs., Part II. and the Staff Manual respectively. Title pages will be prepared in manuscript.

Place	Date	Hour	Summary of Events and Information	Remarks and references to Appendices
NORDAUSQUES	13.2.16		Paid men of section & attached regimental fatigues. Office routine. Lorry arrived & returned to RENINGHELST to fetch remainder of equipment.	
do	14.2.16		To 12 W. YORKS Regt. RECQUES. In majority of billets the shallow french type of latrine is being used. Appears to be satisfactory. Billets are in clean condition; bath have been arranged in a brewery. Suggestion was made to m.o. that water supply should be tested.	
do	15.2.16		Reconnoitred road to AUDRUICQ STATION. Office routine.	
do	16.2.16		Reconnoitred road to ST OMER STATION. Office routine.	
do	17.2.16		Arranged with D.A.Q.M.G. for section of shower baths in Divisional area. Office routine.	

WAR DIARY or INTELLIGENCE SUMMARY

Army Form C. 2118.

of O.C. 5th Sanitary Section, 1st Division

Place	Date	Hour	Summary of Events and Information	Remarks and references to Appendices
NORDAUSQUES	18.2.16		To 23rd & 30th Bdes R.F.A. to arrange for detailing of squads to assist in cleaning up of billets - general sanitary work. Office routine.	
do	19.2.16		To NOTRE DAME Farm to inspect shower bath but found that this has not yet been fitted up. Billets of Div. Grenade School were in satisfactory state.	
do	20.2.16		To 4th ROYAL FUSILIERS at POLINCOVE. Billets are in clean condition. At one billet it was found that refuse was being deposited in an open pit. W.O. agrees that proper trap should be constructed.	
do	21.2.16		To 8th R.E., YORKS at NORTHLEULINGHEM. Billets are in clean condition. Soakpit water from baths is being poured on the ground which has become saturated. O.C. R.E. soil is fairly absorbent. It was suggested that two pits should be constructed, one smaller pit of billets with clinker leading into a larger covered in soakage pit. The neuralin- at A Coy billets requires rebuilding. Same pits left by previous division required filling in. N.C.O. i/c. was instructed to clean up posts billets	

WAR DIARY or INTELLIGENCE SUMMARY

Army Form C. 2118.

O.C. 57 Sanitary Section
II Division

Place	Date	Hour	Summary of Events and Information	Remarks and references to Appendices
NORDAUSQUES	22.2.16		To 30th Bde R.F.A. TOURNEHEM. Inspected H.Q. + Amm. Column billets, also attached Trench Mortar Battery. Billets are in clean condition. Both have been filled up + waste water is drained away through gravel into the river. Office routine.	
do	23.2.16		Reconnoitred road to WIZERNE STATION. Office routine.	
do	24.2.16		To 8th Bde H.Q. EPERLECQUES to inspect Thresh disinfector. Office routine.	
do	25.2.16		To 129th + 130th Batterys (30th Bde R.F.A.) TOURNEHEM. Billets are in clean condition; some are being abandoned owing to snow driving in through the roof. Coolhurse refuse is collected + disposed of to farmers. One latrine erected in narrow passage between two horse lines. One is unsatisfactory position + was suggested that the latrine sheds be removed to an adjoining field. Office routine.	

WAR DIARY or INTELLIGENCE SUMMARY.

Army Form C. 2118.

of No. 5A Sanitary Section III Division

(Erase heading not required.)

Place	Date	Hour	Summary of Events and Information	Remarks and references to Appendices
NORDAUSQUES	26.2.16		Arranged for disinfection & cleaning up of billets in which 8th Bde moving out to. 2nd Royal Scots billets was went to deft sanit. inspection was abandoned. Office routine.	
do	27.2.16		Paid men of section & attached regimental fatigues. To 23rd Bde R.F.A. at BONNINGUES-les-ARDRES to arrange for detailing of men from section to assist in sanitary work. Office routine.	
do	28.2.16		To EPERLECQUES. 8th Bde H.Q. to arrange for future movements & disinfection. Peeling in various points of discipline contained in Munro R.O. Office routine.	
do	29.2.16		To R.Scott Fus at LA PANNE, LE COMMUNAL, LA COMMUNE. Billets were in clean condition. Cookhouses refuse in all billets was being fed to pigs. Excreta & urine are being buried. Water supply appeared to be satisfactory & it was suggested to R.M.O. that water should be boiled. Office routine.	

3rd Div —

5A Sans Section

March 1916

3

5 Sanitary See
Vol II

WAR DIARY or INTELLIGENCE SUMMARY

O.C. S.A. Sanitary Section Army Form C. 2118.
3rd Division

Place	Date	Hour	Summary of Events and Information	Remarks and references to Appendices
NORDAUSQUES	1.3.16		To EPERLECQUES with 8th [?] of S.R. Bde. Billets were found to be in fairly clean condition and arrangements for incinerating refuse & provision for latrines and disinfection of billets sufficient for present.	
do	2.3.16		To ROYAL SCOTS FUS. at LA PANNE LE COMMUNAL, LA COMMUNE. Billets shelters were fair, satisfactory condition. Water supply was derived from a shallow well with insufficient protection, appeared to be polluted, in addition sent for analysis, but report has not yet been received. Coffee [kitchen?]	

WAR DIARY of O.C. 57 Sanitary Section

INTELLIGENCE SUMMARY

(Erase heading not required.)

Army Form C. 2118.

Place	Date	Hour	Summary of Events and Information	Remarks and references to Appendices
NORDAUSQUES	3.3.16		To 1st NORTH'D FUS. at HOUELE. In absence of M.O. inspection was made with sanitary NCO. Billets, latrines & general sanitary arrangements appeared to be satisfactory. Inspected home billets of 8th Bn. at EPERLECQUES. Found that they had been cleaned up & were being disinfected. Office routine.	
do	4.3.16		Inspected billets formerly occupied by battalions of 16th K.R.R. Terms that all rubbish had been burnt & pumes, pits, urine wastes & billets generally in clean & tidy condition. Office [?]	
do	5.3.16		Paid men of section. Attended regimental fatigue. Office routine.	
do	6.3.16		Preparation for divisional gymk[?]. Arranged for division's[?] sectional equipment also for funeral of [?] Bn. 18st Batt. [?]	

WAR DIARY A.D. of Sanitary Section

or

INTELLIGENCE SUMMARY.

Army Form C. 2118.

III Division

(Erase heading not required.)

Place	Date	Hour	Summary of Events and Information	Remarks and references to Appendices
[Field]	7.3.16		Divisional move to RENINGHELST. Took over from 9th Bath. F.S. Saw Lee. I.M.K. Div.	
RENINGHELST	8.3.16		Stocktaking of sundry stables. Arrange for starting work ones for completion of new palons of baths. Building Office routine.	
do	9.3.16		To I + J camps. These camps appear to be in an unsanitary condition. Great quantities of rubbish has accumulated round all incinerators, two in working order, & there having been broken down. Many of the ditches & drains containing food & refuse & drain in vicinity of latrines were full of urine. Apparently each camp was occupied by parties of three Battalions. Two M.O.s & two sanitary men were interviewed & states that all Battalions were moving out on the last day but they would clear up as much as possible. Basin of ablution bench in J camp were choked & the corkhouses were in an unsanitary state in both camps. Office routine.	

WAR DIARY

f. O.C. 67 Sanitary Section Army Form C. 2118.

III Division.

INTELLIGENCE SUMMARY

(Erase heading not required.)

Place	Date	Hour	Summary of Events and Information	Remarks and references to Appendices
RENINGHELST	10.3.16		Arranges for disinfection of billets at DICKEBUSCH + spraying of huts in Bn. area. To D camp. Incinerator has been broken down & a quantity of rubbish has accumulated. Owing in recent frost have put latrines with refuse & boundary ditch of camp entirely into this [frozen?] + in some places solid. As the camp was proceeding 2 Inde: were detailed from attached unit of section to commence cleaning up the refuse, ice moveables - start burning rubbish. Details given for sanitary work on T.J. camp. To E camp. This camp appeared to be in a fairly satisfactory condition, but was still in occupation [by?] of the units of the 19th Div.	
do	11.3.16		To 8th Bde H.Q. + adjoining camps. The camp was temporarily occupied by 2 ROYAL SCOTS. The camp was being cleaned up + rubbish burnt as rapidly as possible. The ditch on E. side of camp contains a quantity of tins, grease + refuse of same form. [Recommend?] reforming latrine. The pans on W. side of camp. + transforming lines.	

WAR DIARY of O.C. 57 Sanitary Section

Army Form C. 2118.

III Division

INTELLIGENCE SUMMARY
(Erase heading not required.)

Place	Date	Hour	Summary of Events and Information	Remarks and references to Appendices
PENINGHELST	11.3.16		Were billeted with two were billeted with two To K camp (opposite windmill on LOCRE ROAD). The camp was in a fairly filthy condition. The incinerator was broken & the horsefall incinerator had apparently been used for general rubbish, rind shelters, milk cans, tins &c. The latrines & urinal were rather foul, faeces & urine on the ground & soiled paper lying about. Details men to rebuild & repair incinerators in W.K. & J camps. Office routine	
do	12.3.16		Paid proper employes in connection with Div. baths. Inspection [bath] by G.O.C. Division & A.A. & Q.M.G. Paid men of section & attached regimental fatigues. Office routine	
do	13.3.16		To BAILLEUL to purchase material. To I & J camps. Found fatigue party 2 R.Scots working in J camp. Section fatigue men in J Camp, collecting rubbish, cleaning out drains & office routine.	

WAR DIARY of O.C. SA Sanitary Section Army Form C. 2118.
or
INTELLIGENCE SUMMARY.

(Erase heading not required.)

III Division

Instructions regarding War Diaries and Intelligence Summaries are contained in F. S. Regs., Part II. and the Staff Manual respectively. Title pages will be prepared in manuscript.

Place	Date	Hour	Summary of Events and Information	Remarks and references to Appendices
RENINGHELST	14.3.16		Inspection Khaki Dry DAQMG. Canadian Div. & Officer i/c Sanitary Section Canadian Corps. To A camp. Majority of rubbish in camp has been collected into tins heaps but extra amount was still lying about - awaiting collection. NCO i/c reported that latrine tins been left in an insanitary condition that feces has been found in many parts of the camp, but that these has all been cleaned up & buried. The site of the Old camp was also in an insanitary condition - mainly that the tents contained its clothing, stale food &c. Official routine.	M.M.
do	15.3.16		To B camp (SHORL) Camp was fairly free from rubbish. Ground in vicinity of latrine was very foul with urine & urinal rubbish. In various parts of camp requires burning & latrines required cleaning out. N.O. & Q.M. were both informed & latter that fatigue parties were being put on to clean up.	

1577 Wt.W10791/1773 500,000 1/15 D. D. & L. A.D.S.S./Forms/C. 2118.

WAR DIARY or INTELLIGENCE SUMMARY

Army Form C. 2118.

(Erase heading not required.)

F.O.C. Sanitary Section — III Division

Place	Date	Hour	Summary of Events and Information	Remarks and references to Appendices
RENINGHELST	15.3.16 (cont)		Interviews with O.C. Sanitary Section III Division (Canadian). Officer posted sick.	
do	16.3.16		To D.I.J. camp: large trench latrine has been newly dug & both camps turning & burying rubbish pits & camps are now in fairly clean condition. Incinerators have been rebuilt. Attention drawn to No. 3 & E. YORKS in Green to the prone site in 1 camp which was unsatisfactory (1 Regiment using 6 first side, the shannon at the ablution bench 900 per line) Dalmands.	
			16 E camp: This camp is in fairly clean condition two unoccupied at time of inspection. The private lat. at the latrine was overflowing & required shifting. Rather a large amount of unburnt rubbish has been left round incinerators where was a small amount of general rubbish in some of the ditches & along boundaries of camps.	
			To Transport lines of 1st R.S. Fusiliers & 3.3. YORKS. The incinerators in	

WAR DIARY of A.D.C. Sanitary Section III Division

INTELLIGENCE SUMMARY

Place	Date	Hour	Summary of Events and Information	Remarks and references to Appendices
RENINGHELST	16.3.16 (cont)		R.S.I. hut has been broken down & a quantity of rubbish had accumulated. Latrines were in a satisfactory condition. Tea leaves & refuse from mess tins has been scattered round the steam from which supply of water for cooking purpose is obtained. Attention of A.D.S. was drawn to these defects & instructions given to sanitary N.C.O. to have been remedied. The manure from the horse lines in R.S.I. camp is disposed of to farmers. Office routine.	
do	17.3.16		To B camp to attend held Genl. Court Martial. Owing to non arrival of witnesses court martial was postponed at 4 P.M. Inspection of baths by A.D.M.S. 3rd Canadian Division. Office routine.	
do	18.3.16		To B camp. To Y.G.C.M. Inspected various H.Q. offices in RENINGHELST:— C.R.A.; G.J. Office; M. Police. This have little variation latrines at Signal office, Sawmill &c. An N.Co. fatigue party has	

WAR DIARY or INTELLIGENCE SUMMARY

Army Form C. 2118.

D.O.C. 57 Sanitary Section
III Division

Place	Date	Hour	Summary of Events and Information	Remarks and references to Appendices
PENINGHELST	18.3.16 (contd)		been detailed for work on H.Q. Offices + at time of inspection these were all in fairly satisfactory condition. Office routine.	
do	19.3.16		Drew 3000 francs in respect a/c. Pay women employed in connection with Div. Laundry & Bath. Inspection of bath by various members of Canadian medical service attached regimental fatigues. Office routine. Paid men of section.	
do	20.3.16		To METEREN to inspect hole of 3rd Canadian Divsion. Arranges for disinfection of accumulated horse manure in Divisional area. Office Routine.	
do	21.3.16		To A camp. Inspected camp with N.O. of 10R WELCH FUSILIERS. Work has been going on continuously in connection with cleaning up this camp. An incinerator has been erected + a large amount of rubbish disposed of but a fair amount still remains to be	

Army Form C. 2118.

WAR DIARY of No. 3 Sanitary Section
III Division
INTELLIGENCE SUMMARY
(Erase heading not required.)

Place	Date	Hour	Summary of Events and Information	Remarks and references to Appendices
RENINGHELST	21.3.16 (cont)		Leaves, not especially on the old camp site where the publicat is very muddy & scattered. At the time of inspection work has been interrupted to settle all tent in camp owing to recent shelling. To camp of 4 YORKS & LANCS. This camp is in a very good condition. Drains have been dug underneath all the duck board. The urinoirs has been covered in, & a new grease trap constructed. A fresh urine pit had been dug at end of latrine. As the ground must the latrine has become rather foul it was suggested that the floor should be bricked. The latrine seats has become rather worn, being renewed & it was suggested that - a urine soak should be fitted to front of seats. Excreta is being burnt. The stance at the ablution bench appears to be inadequate & suggestions were made for improvement. From to SK Isle H.Q. camp. This appears to be in satisfactory condition. Instructions were given for filling & cleaning the ablution layer. Detailed N.C.O. for sanitary work in the Belgian Battery Office conduit.	

WAR DIARY
or
INTELLIGENCE SUMMARY.

O.C. 57 Sanitary Section, III Division — Army Form C. 2118.

Place	Date	Hour	Summary of Events and Information	Remarks and references to Appendices
RENINGHELST	22.3.16		35 men of No. 8. F.A. detailed for work under Section NCOs in connection with treatment of horse manure in transport wagon lines of divisional units. Visited transport lines of various units during morning to supervise work. To BEDFORD HOUSE in connection with lecture on "sanitation". Office routine in afternoon.	
do	23.3.16		Prepared lecture. To POPERINGHE (Officers School of Instruction) in afternoon. Owing to entrain in date, lecture postponed. Office routine.	
do	24.3.16		To 30th Bde R.F.A. Inspected Bde HQ, Amm. Column, 129th & 130th Batteries. H.Q. F.A.C. were in a fairly satisfactory condition. A certain amount of rubbish still remains to be cleared away but this is being disposed of as rapidly as possible. All excreta is burnt. Some small sheds used by officers servants were in an unsanitary condition, rubbish, scraps of food re lying about. Instructions were given for this to be cleared up. 129 + 130th 15th Bties these huts are in an unexpectedly muddy state but are themselves in a fairly satisfactory condition. The huts are partited in a very unde area	

WAR DIARY

INTELLIGENCE SUMMARY

A.C. 5A Sanitary Section Army Form C. 2118.
III Division.

Place	Date	Hour	Summary of Events and Information	Remarks and references to Appendices
RENINGHELST	24.3.16 (contd)		but sycrete is being burnt — in brick destructors. All cookhouse refuse is being burnt or thrown through grease traps. Refuse was found in ditches outside several huts — attention being directed to this. To E camp. The urine pit at the latrine was found to be overflowing & ground in vicinity becoming very foul. The camp was occupied at time of inspection by 4 R. Fusiliers. Attention of N.C.O. was drawn to this & it was suggested that urine should be caught in a bucket & disposed of in a grease pit until urinal could be made to new site. The ground in the vicinity of the incinerator was in a very untidy condition, tins & general rubbish being scattered about. Excreta & coarse cookhouse refuse is being burnt. Liquid refuse from cookhouse strained through grease trap. To divisional transport camp on N.E. side of E camp. This also has been conferences but no latrines, horse standings & several tents & miscellaneous shelters still remain. As latrines & shelters were still being used casually, remainder was disinfected. To clear the site. Camps were left in very untidy state but all rubbish has been collected by fatigue squad from section office routine.	

WAR DIARY or INTELLIGENCE SUMMARY

Army Form C.2118.

of N.C. 5th Sanitary Section, II Division

Place	Date	Hour	Summary of Events and Information	Remarks and references to Appendices
RENINGHELST	25.3.16		To 4R, 5R, 7BR Belgian Battery line at DICKEBUSCH. An N.C.O. from section has been detailed for sanitary supervision of the regt. Latrines has been erected in all batteries. Two incinerators and one latrine seat in the 4R, 5R, 6R Battery + an additional trench in the 5R Battery. Drinking water is obtained from tanks at DICKEBUSCH. A considerable quantity of manure has accumulated in vicinity of horse standings & will be either burned as soon as material are available — Cookhouse refuse is being burned but will be burned as soon as incinerators are available. Some of the men are occupying small huts & a very unsatisfactory nature built of material salvage from YPRES. To D camp the latrine has been moved to a more convenient site at E. end of camp. Urinal in N.C.O.'s latrine was too small + appears to be unnecessary. In absence of any instructions were given for its removal. Line was no drain at the altitude bench Hedge n N. side of camp was in a very unitary state his + general rubbish scattered along help. un boundary ditch. The oles formerly occupied by cookhouse was also very unitidy with emigates pure, drains	

1577 Wt.W10791/1773 500,000 1/15 D.D. & L. A.D.S.S./Forms/C. 2118.

WAR DIARY or INTELLIGENCE SUMMARY

Army Form C. 2118.

Loc. SA Sanitary Section
III Division.

Place	Date	Hour	Summary of Events and Information	Remarks and references to Appendices
RENINGHELST	25.3.16 (cont'd)		Oven & still remaining under has suddenly been emptying made his between some of the huts, in addition to throwing out other rubbish. Instructions were given for receptacles to be placed near huts. By the grease trap at the cookhouse entrance no draining material. In officers camp cookhouse refuse was being burned. Instructions given for pit to be taken to incinerator in main camp. The whole camp is being cleaned up & rapidly on trouble. To "I.W.L.I" & "N. Fus." transport lines. Flea appears to be in satisfactory condition. Manure is being carted away by farmers. Latrine in K.S.L.I. lines, figure moving to fresh site as ground has become rather foul. There was no change at Abeelion trenches in N. Fus. lines. Office routine.	
do	26.3.16.		Figures 5000 for in respect of Paid women employed in connection with Div. Bath, laundry, Baths men & section. Inspected huts & camp site. office routine.	

WAR DIARY
INTELLIGENCE SUMMARY

Army Form C. 2118.

of O.C. 5A Sanitary Section
3rd Division

Place	Date	Hour	Summary of Events and Information	Remarks and references to Appendices
RENINGHELST	21.3.16		To K camp (16th Bde M. Gun Coy). At time of inspection camp was being cleared up by fatigue party working under two R.A.M.C. orderlies attached to the M.G. Coy. The boundary ditches of the camp were in an insanitary condition, tins & other refuse having been deposited therein. Excreta was being buried. Instructions were given for it to be burnt in Horsfall destructor. Urine pit was overflowing & directions were given for removal of urinal to fresh site. A grease trap was needed at the cookhouse. Washing arrangements at ablution bench were inadequate. Instructions were given for removal of sundry drains, enclosures & shelters. To E camp. An additional incinerator was required to deal with rubbish from camp. Faeces are being burnt but are mixed with sawdust on the ground. Instructions were given for covered receptacles to be obtained for the purpose. Sanitary men was instructed to shift urinal to fresh position. Details man from section to burn incinerator. To H camp. Camp at time of inspection was occupied by 10 R.W. Fus. General receptacle for urine needed for missing faecets sawdust. Latrine required removing to	

WAR DIARY

A.D.S.S. Somebody? Sector 3rd Division
Army Form C. 2118.

INTELLIGENCE SUMMARY

(Erase heading not required.)

Place	Date	Hour	Summary of Events and Information	Remarks and references to Appendices
RENINGHELST	27.3.16 (contd)		first aid convoy is grand having become fixed. Office routine.	
do	28.3.16		To water tanks at ABEELE. Water is rather muddy but otherwise quality appears to be satisfactory. Passed men of attached regimental fatigues. Office routine.	
do	29.3.16		To reservoir on MONT ROUGE. Inspected catchment area. This is very muddy, but otherwise in fairly satisfactory condition. To 42nd Bde R.F.A. H.Q. Ammn. Column. 29 k. Sty waggon being rapidly assembled. Mobile Disinfector away being carted, a depot of a quantity of linen, which has accumulated in 29 & 15th lines.	

Army Form C. 2118.

WAR DIARY Field Ambulance ......
or
INTELLIGENCE SUMMARY. 3rd Division

(Erase heading not required.)

Place	Date	Hour	Summary of Events and Information	Remarks and references to Appendices
RENINGHELST	30.3.16		To METEREN to arrange for billets for section + attached fatigue men/ Inspected Interviews with O.C. & enquired water Patrol with reference to disposal of waste bath water in new area. Two N.C.O.s details for examination of water supplies in VOORMEZEELE.	
do	31.3.16		Visit from O.C. Canadian C.A.M.C. Bath. Arrangements for handing over baths to General Standing work & office routine	

R.W. Matheson
Capt RAMC
O.C. Sanitary Sec 3rd Dn

WAR DIARY

of

No. 5a. Sanitary Section 3rd Division ? Cav Div

for

April 1916

COMMITTEE FOR THE
MEDICAL HISTORY OF THE WAR

Date   9-JUN.1916

Confidential

A.G's Office
G.H.Q. 3rd Echelon

Please find attached the War Diary of S.A. Section 1st London Sanitary Company R.a.m.c.(T.F.) for month of April 1916.
(7 Enclosures)

4/5/16.

A. Nicol.
Capt. R.a.m.c.
for A.D.M.S.
3rd Divn.

Vol. III

WAR DIARY of O.C. SA Sanitary Section Army Form C. 2118.
INTELLIGENCE SUMMARY. 2nd Division.

(Erase heading not required.)

Place	Date	Hour	Summary of Events and Information	Remarks and references to Appendices
RENINGHELST	1.4.16		To 41st & 45th Btties. R.F.A. Billets were in very huddly condition. General sanitary arrangements satisfactory. Excreta is being burnt. Arrangements for move. Office routine.	RJW
do	2.4.16		To X Coast army to complaint of O.C. 2 Canadian Fld. Coy. Opened new cookhouse, prevented midday. Steward canteen & latrines in satisfactory condition. Paid promenade employees in connection with Bde laundry. Also men of section. & attached regimental fatigues. Office routine.	RJW
do	3.4.16		Handed over to Sanr. Sec. 2nd Can. Div. Inspected hut lines with O.C. 2nd Bde. Can. Sanders.	RJW
do	4.4.16		To camps in area with O.C. Sanders. 2nd Can. Div.	RJW
do	5.4.16		Handed over Baths & Laundry to 2nd Can. Div.	RJW

WAR DIARY

Army Form C. 2118.

f. O.C. SA Sanitary Section
3rd Division

(Erase heading not required.)

Place	Date	Hour	Summary of Events and Information	Remarks and references to Appendices
RENINGHELST	6.4.16		Moved to METEREN.	
METEREN	7.4.16		To A.D.M.S. + Q Office. Arranges for starting staff. Details men for working in new area. Arranges billets for section + attached men.	
do	8.4.16		To A.D.M.S. + Q Office. To BAILLEUL. Drew 3000 fr on account a/c Pay. Section + attached men reg'l fatigue. Office routine.	
do	9.4.16		To RENINGHELST to lend personal influence to (1 or 3) Brit Laundry to clear up Study matters in connection with Sanitary work Staff.	
do	10.4.16		To A.D.M.S. re question of allied RAMC men for Sanitary work. Arranges officer, water supply from METEREN. Men for fetching supplies in BM area. Office routine.	

WAR DIARY or INTELLIGENCE SUMMARY.

Army Form C. 2118.

Place	Date	Hour	Summary of Events and Information	Remarks and references to Appendices
METEREN	11.4.16		To Bn HdQ HQ. MONT DES CATS. To 12 W. YORKS billets. Found shallow French type of latrine in use owing to lack of latrine pans & to difficulty for latrine incinerator. Arranged for burning of faeces. Office wire.	
do	12.4.16		To ARMY. Gave evidence at Gen. Court Martial METEREN.	
do	13.4.16		To ABLUS & Q Office. To 4th R.FUSILIERS. Found men in WNYC company washing. All ponds owing to lack of ablution benches. Insufficient fire material for latrines & ablution keeps. Ordered two re building of faeces & necessity for ablution benches. Office routine.	
do	14.4.16		To ADMS. Interview with DW Drainage Officer. Considered of report by V Corps water boring meeting re water supplies in new area.	
do	15.4.16		Reconnoitred road to CASSEL. To Bn baths & arranged for purification of route water. Detailed scrimy parties to clean out billets. Lieu FLETCHER	

WAR DIARY or INTELLIGENCE SUMMARY.

Army Form C. 2118.

A.D.C. Sanitary Section 3rd Division

(Erase heading not required.)

Place	Date	Hour	Summary of Events and Information	Remarks and references to Appendices
METEREN	16.4.16		Inspected transport camp (Ammunition - Supply Col. & various Divnl.) in METEREN - FLETRE road. Arranged with officer i/c Q.M.S's for burning of faeces. To A.D.M.S. & M.O. i/c 10 R.W.Fusiliers. Discussed points re sanitary of site of Australian transport camp. Office routine.	R/M
do	17.4.16		Conference with Div. Drainage officer re employment of Special Sanitary Squad detailed for pioneering duties. Office routine.	R/M
do	18.4.16		To 8.E.Yorks billet. Grease trap. Latrine inconvenient in unsatisfactory state owing to lack of hut. Officer to supply him from dump. Sgt METEREN. To A.D.M.S. Office & on work.	R/M
do	19.4.16		To WESTOUTRE. Inspection laundry & baths. Also baths at LOCRE & LA CLYTTE	R/M

WAR DIARY
INTELLIGENCE SUMMARY

of O.C. Sanitary Section 3rd Division

Army Form C. 2118.

Place	Date	Hour	Summary of Events and Information	Remarks and references to Appendices
METEREN	20.4.16		To WESTOUTRE. Inspected new Div. area with O.C. Sanitary Section 50th Div.	
do	21.4.16		Took over area with O.C. Sanitary 50th Div. Inspection of baths by o/c baths 50th Div.	
do	22.4.16		To I.R.S. FUSILIERS billets. Latrines are being burned. This has been fairly efficient. Water s/s for un-infested a/c. from METEREN. To BAILLEUL. Brew 300 f—	
do	23.4.16		To 7th S.L.I. billets, BERTHEN. These were left in fairly clean condition. Some accumulation of rubbish was noticeable. Also in connection with laundry. Also one of section attached to latrines. Office routine.	
do	24.4.16		To 40th Bde. R.F.A. at EECKE. Manure is being drained of to farmers. Office routine.	

WAR DIARY or INTELLIGENCE SUMMARY

Army Form C. 2118.

(Erase heading not required.)

Place	Date	Hour	Summary of Events and Information	Remarks and references to Appendices
METEREN	25.4.16		To WESTOUTRE in various parties (mounted) with mule in new area. Office routine	BPM BPM
do	26.4.16		Moved to WESTOUTRE	BPM
WESTOUTRE	27.4.16		Started baths at LOCRE. ADMS & Q officer to LOCRE & LA CLYTTE. Cleared laundry for work. To LOCRE & LA CLYTTE in connection with attention to S.S.O. to arrange for coal supply. Arranged for collection of refuse from billets & cookhouses. LOCRE Offd routine	BPM
do	28.4.16		To LOCRE. Inspected 13 W. YORKS Camp. Arranged with two ??? hospital & laundry. Arranged to hire site owing to position of farm by occupation of water. Quantity manure awaiting removal in farmyard below. Also an open burnt cookhouse that burnt on farm is fife to life at LOCRE & LA CLYTTE in connection with inspection of farm west water	

WAR DIARY

for- S.Sanitary Section 33 Division

INTELLIGENCE SUMMARY

Army Form C. 2118.

Place	Date	Hour	Summary of Events and Information	Remarks and references to Appendices
WESTOUTRE	28.4.16 (contd)		To 1. GORDONS camp LOCRE. Camp is in fairly clean condition. Faeces are not being burnt. Two urinals that sawdust-ends be obtained from R.E. dump. Quantity of rubbish left by outgoing unit is being burnt in trenches. Office routine.	SMN
do	29.4.16		To 5.R Northumn. Fus (50th Div) at LOCRE. & 8 K.O.R.L. Faeces are being burnt at both. To Baths at LOCRE & LA CLYTTE. To various R.E. dumps. M.T. redress at LOCRE. Office routine.	SMN
do	30.4.16		To Various units & H.Q's. To Div H.Q WESTOUTRE. Arrange for collection & incineration of rubbish at LOCRE from billets & cookhouses. Various units in connection with laundry sheets. Office routine.	SMN

No. 5 a Sanitary Section

May 1916

WAR DIARY for Stanley Sections
INTELLIGENCE SUMMARY. 3rd Div.

Army Form C. 2118.

Place	Date	Hour	Summary of Events and Information	Remarks and references to Appendices
WESTOUTRE	1.5.16		To ADMS & Q. Office. To CRE. to arrange for various alterations & additions to bath & laundry. To LOCRE to see ls. Batt. Inspected camp of 13th K. KINGS (L'POOL) Regt. with M.O. Office routine. SMc	
do	2.5.16		To LA CLYTTE. Inspected huts. To water supply on LA CLYTTE - KEMMEL ROAD. Inspected camp of 1st ENTRENCHING BATTALION. LA CLYTTE. To LOCRE Inspected camp of 10th R.W.F. detail. Office routine	
do	3.5.16		To ADMS - Q Office. To CRE - DADOS. To water supply on LOCRE - BAILLEUL ROAD. Inspected magazine lines of N. IRISH HORSE & magn lines of 40th Bde R.F.A. Interviews with D.D.O. & OC Corps water Boring Office routine	

Army Form C. 2118.

WAR DIARY
No. 5. A Sanitary Section E.D. DIV.

INTELLIGENCE SUMMARY.

(Erase heading not required.)

Place	Date	Hour	Summary of Events and Information	Remarks and references to Appendices
Westoutre	4/5/16		Office routine. Inspected Laundry, Westoutre. Visited and inspected Love baths and water supply on Loore Bailleul road.	
	5/5/16		Office routine. Inspected baths and Laundry, Westoutre, went to office and A.D.M.S. Office. Paid visit to A.D.S. & sew-baths. Paid visit Loore, and new baths. Inspected 9th Bde. M.G. Coy billets, about which there had been a complaint from A.D.M.S. Coy. attached. Barn stuffy, but no unusual features about it. Camp in fairly good condition.	
	6/5/16		Office work. Baths and Laundry at Westoutre A.D.M.S. Office & chief work. Began to construct tanks for disposal of office & W.C. own firstly water. Inspected new camp, new officers latrine.	
	7/5/16		Baths at Loore. Office. Began to construct new dressing room at Loore.	
	8/5/16		Office work. Inspected baths at La Clytte, and visited camp of I. Entrenching Battalion. Camp was very clean and well kept. Fires are disposed of by burning. Water supply from a stream; but water is thoroughly boiled. Latrine was in rather close proximity to a drain leading from a stagnant pond.	

Army Form C. 2118.

WAR DIARY for S-4 Sanitary
or Section. B.N. Div.
INTELLIGENCE SUMMARY.

(Erase heading not required.)

Place	Date	Hour	Summary of Events and Information	Remarks and references to Appendices
Westoutre	9/5/16		Office work. A.D.M.S. Office. Baths and Laundry, Westoutre. Inspected baths at Locre.	
	10/5/16		Office work. Q. Office. Inspected baths and Laundry.	
	11/5/16		Went round with D.A.D.M.S.	
	12/5/16		Office work. Inspected baths at Westoutre, La Clytte and Locre. R.E. office and Q. Office re Laundry flooring.	
	13/5/16		Routine work. Baths at Locre. Q.W. Office.	
	14/5/16		Office work. Inspected Laundry and Baths at Westoutre. Routine work.	

Army Form C. 2118.

WAR DIARY of O.C. SA Sanitary Section
or 3rd Division
INTELLIGENCE SUMMARY.

(Erase heading not required.)

Instructions regarding War Diaries and Intelligence Summaries are contained in F. S. Regs., Part II. and the Staff Manual respectively. Title pages will be prepared in manuscript.

Place	Date	Hour	Summary of Events and Information	Remarks and references to Appendices
WESTOUTRE	15/5/16		To Q. office & A.D.M.S. Interviews with Div. Drainage Officer. Inspected baths & laundry at WESTOUTRE, baths at LOCRE, LA CLYTTE. Office routine.	SMM
do	16/5/16		To LOCRE. Inspected BADAJOZ HUTS, village & camp of 7K N. Fusiliers. Inspected laundry at WESTOUTRE with A.D.M.S. To CRE re alterations, laundry & baths & disinfectors. Baths at laundry. Office routine	SMM
do	17/5/16		To LOCRE. Inspected camp of 2 Suffolks with M.O. Arranged for squad of 15 men from Bri: Drainage Section to move in Suffolks camp. 4500 P(W) women employed in connection with above. Inspected laundry with D.A.Q.M.G. To S.S.O. to arrange for coal supply. Inspected camps of Nos 2 & 4 Corp Bn: Trains. Various matters in connection with baths. Office routine	SMM
do	18/5/16		Preliminary arrangements for bells & chutes at baths laundry. To LOCRE - Inspected huts with D.D.O to chose new site for baths in LOCRE - BAILLEUL Road. To 7K F.Ambulance LOCRE re drainage of laundry at—	

WAR DIARY or INTELLIGENCE SUMMARY

O.C. 5th Sanitary Section, 3rd Division

Place	Date	Hour	Summary of Events and Information	Remarks and references to Appendices
WESTOUTRE	18.8.16 (contd)		To water supply at LOCRE. Inspected reservoir. To Q. Office. Arranged for cleaning out of water tank at RIDGE WOOD. Office routine.	
do	19.8.16		Inspection of laundry, baths & sundry camps with A.A. & Q.M.G. 69th Bn. To LOCRE to various camps in 76th BDE area. Arranged for squads to be detailed from Fwd. Drainage Squad for work on chlorination tanks at LA CLYTTE & LOCRE. Office routine.	
do	20.8.16		To C.R.E. re various matters in connection with laundry, baths. Paid men employed at baths & camps [LA CLYTTE. Inspected camps of 11th [Argyll & Sutherland]; 7 K.S.L.I.; 1 R.S.F.; 2 R. Scots & E. Yorks; 7 K.S.L.I.; 1 R.S.F.; 2 R. Scots. Bath, transport camps of R. Scots & 7th Field Coy. R.E.; 250th Tunn. Coy. R.E. also camps of Cheshire F. Coy R.E. All near LA CLYTTE. Office routine.	
do	21.8.16		Paid men employed at WESTOUTRE. To METEREN to O/C baths & D.C. Sanitary 50th Division. Office routine.	

WAR DIARY

O.C. SA SANITARY Section Army Form C. 2118.
By A Warren

INTELLIGENCE SUMMARY.

(Erase heading not required.)

Place	Date	Hour	Summary of Events and Information	Remarks and references to Appendices
WESTOUTRE	22.5.16		To LOCRE. Paid men employed at bath camps. To laundry re disinfection work. To ADOS & Office. Infected camp for 20 in K.R. Rifles. To LOCRE to arrange for bath in, drainage by in. Infects camp of 10 R.W. Fusiliers. Squad details for sanitary work at VIERSTRAAT. Office routine	SW
do	23/6/16		To CRE & Q office. To LOCRE re disinfection. To LA CYTTE - KEMMEL roads. Arranged for refixing of supply in LA CYTTE. In. Drainage section. Infects R.E. drain by squad from Infects (St R. Cay R.E.) (Infects) R.C. Fuzs. + SIEGE F-AAPA (Can. Rullers) 12 W. Yorks). Office routine	SW
do	24/5/16		Visit from O. Sanzler. Offices re bath SDR Din. To LA CYTTE re disinfectors baths + disinfection huts. Office routine	SW

Army Form C. 2118.

WAR DIARY of O.C. SA Sanitary Section
or
INTELLIGENCE SUMMARY. 3D Division.

(Erase heading not required.)

Place	Date	Hour	Summary of Events and Information	Remarks and references to Appendices
WESTOUTRE	25.5.16		To METEREN to arrange billets. Office routine	
do	26.5.16		To LOCRE. Inspected bath & KEMMEL SHELTERS. To ADMS, Q Office. Arrangements for men & Laundry & Div. Drainage Squad. Office routine. Paid women employed at Laundry.	SM SM SM
do	27.5.16		Moves to METEREN	
METEREN	28.5.16		To ADMS & Q Office at FLETRE. Inspected baths. Arranged work of Div. Drainage Squad. Office routine	SM
do	29.5.16		To Q Office FLETRE re transport arrangements for washing. Interview with O.C. 7th Labour Battn. Various work connected with Baths, Sanitation, Drainage. Office routine	SM

WAR DIARY or INTELLIGENCE SUMMARY

Army Form C. 2118.

Place	Date	Hour	Summary of Events and Information	Remarks and references to Appendices
METEREN	30.8.16		To 4th ROYAL FUSILIER billets METEREN. Inspected billets with M.O. Interview with Officer i/c baths. Sick Bay. Office work. 8 Un	
do	31.8.16		To 12th W. YORKS Regt at ST JANS CAPPEL. Paid men Speeches. To APPVE. 8 Un	

R.J. Mathews.
Capt RAMC
OC Sanitary Section 2nd Army

SECRET

WAR DIARY of
O.C. 5A Sanitary Section 3rd Division

JUNE 1916.

COMMITTEE FOR THE
MEDICAL HISTORY OF THE WAR
Date 31 AUG. 1916

J.W. Mathews
Capt. RAMC
O.C. Sa. Sec.
3rd Div

WAR DIARY

of O.C. SA Sanitary Section
3rd Division

Army Form C. 2118.

INTELLIGENCE SUMMARY.

(Erase heading not required.)

Place	Date	Hour	Summary of Events and Information	Remarks and references to Appendices
METEREN.	1.6.16		To 4th ROYAL FUSILIERS. Inspected company billet, transport lines with M.O. To Q office to A.D.M.S. Office routine. 8hm	
do	2.6.16		To 12th W.YORKS near BAILLEUL. Inspected company HQ billets. To baths re disinfection of mens baths. Office routine. 8hm	
do	3.6.16		To Q office enquiring disposal mens clothing. Inspected various water supplies near METEREN. Bn. HQ. office at FLETRE Inspected. Office routine. 8hm	
do	4.6.16		To A.D.M.S. Interview with acting O.C. Sewer. 24th Division. 30 T.U. men returned to units. 8hm	
do	5.6.16		Inspected billets of 2. R. SCOTS with M.O. To BAILLEUL to draw 5000 faces on impost life. Paris attacked men of section. 8hm	

WAR DIARY or INTELLIGENCE SUMMARY.

{ O.C. 5A Sanitary Section 3rd Division }

Army Form C. 2118.

(Erase heading not required.)

Place	Date	Hour	Summary of Events and Information	Remarks and references to Appendices
METEREN	6.6.16		Inspected billets of 13 Kings (Liverpool) Regt. near BAILLEUL. Inspected billets of 7th Labour Batt. Office routine.	
do	7.6.16		To FLETRE. To Q & ADMS, D.A.D.O.S. Paid women employed by baths in METEREN district. Office routine.	
do	8.6.16		Inspected billets of 10 R. Welch Fus. Paid women in FLETRE district. Office routine.	
do	9.6.16		To WESTOUTRE to Dr. 50th Div. lab. To baths at METEREN re clarification of sundry matters. Office routine.	
do	10.6.16		To FLETRE. Inspected Div. H.Q., Salvage Coy. To Q Office. Paid women in MT DES CATS & SCHAEXKEN district. Office routine. Office routine.	

# WAR DIARY or INTELLIGENCE SUMMARY

Army Form C. 2118.

(Erase heading not required.)

Place	Date	Hour	Summary of Events and Information	Remarks and references to Appendices
METEREN	11.6.16		To BOESCHEPPE to inspect 85. Yorks billets. Pass men. Section. Office routine.	
do	12.6.16		To bath. Inspected billets of YKSLI near BERTHEN. To BADOS FLETRE. Office routine	
do	13.6.16		To FLETRE to Q office & DDO. To bath. re Clarification. In afternoon to FLETRE to ADMS. Arranges for evacuation of sick. Office routine	
do	14.6.16		To baths. To 3rd Bn Supply Col workshops BAILLEUL re today. That disinfector. Inspects HQ Coy Bn Train FLETRE. To ADMS & DDO Office routine	
do	15.6.16		To bath. To No 4 Coy Bn Train. Interviews with MO. To FLETRE to ADMS & Q office. Interviews with OC 13 King's Liverpool Regt. Office routine	

WAR DIARY or INTELLIGENCE SUMMARY

Army Form C. 2118.

5A Sanitary Section 3rd Division.

Place	Date	Hour	Summary of Events and Information	Remarks and references to Appendices
METEREN	16.6.16		To baths. To Q Office to arrange for transfer of clothing to 24th Division. Arranged to bathe 1st Bn. N.F. To 9.D.N.S. & transfer of linen that disinfect. Paid women employed in connection with Div. Laundry. Office routine. SLM	
do	17.6.16		To C.R.S. & Camp commandant re Div. move. Clothing collected from bathe by 24th Div. To BAILLEUL. To BAILLEUL to DADSOS re Div. arrangements for Div. move. Office routine. SLM	
do	18.6.16		Marches from METEREN to WEMARS-CAPPEL. SLM	
do	19.6.16		Marches from WEMARS-CAPPEL to BROXEELE. SLM	
do	20.6.16		Marches from BROXEELE to TILQUES. To Q Office re training. SLM	
TILQUES	21.6.16		To Q Office re training. To METEREN to pay women employed by Laundry. Drew 1500 frs on imprest a/c in BAILLEUL. SLM	

Army Form C. 2118.

WAR DIARY
for SA Sanitary Section
or
3rd Division
INTELLIGENCE SUMMARY.
(Erase heading not required.)

Place	Date	Hour	Summary of Events and Information	Remarks and references to Appendices
TILQUES	22/6/16		To ADMS & Q office re having 4 Foden truck disinfector by 74 F.T.A. 24th Division. To NORDAUSQUES to arrange for section of steam bath. To EPERLECQUES to 26 K Bde HQ to take over HOULLE office routine. 12 TV men returned to battalion.	SWW
do	23/6/16		To Q office, ADMS, DADOS & Div Salvage Officer. To NORDAUSQUES via MOULLE where timber was collected. Shower bath erected. Identification being constructed. Pass attached. Section men now office routine.	SWW
do	24/6/16		To ADMS & Q office. To HOULLE. To baths. Bath at NORDAUSQUES dismantled. Office routine. To EPERLECQUES to receive reports from NCO's i/c section supervising camps of York Bde.	SWW
do	25/6/16		To ADMS. Trial of 3 J. turner. To DADOS, APM, Salvage officer, Gas officer. Routine. Sentence by ADMS: No 4012 L/c BROWN.T. 2 R.Scots. Deprived of one rank 10 days F.P. No 1	SWW

8510 PTE. WILKES.E.J. 2 R. SCOTS
6166 SPR. MARSDEN. E. Re: Compulsory R.S.

Army Form C. 2118.

WAR DIARY of OC. SA Sanitary Section
or
INTELLIGENCE SUMMARY. 3D Division
(Erase heading not required.)

Place	Date	Hour	Summary of Events and Information	Remarks and references to Appendices
TILQUES	26.6.16		To HOULLE in connection with various arrangements for baths. Inspection of T.V. men by ADMS. 9 men returned to duty, viz.	
			7307 Pte McDERMID. R. 1st GORDONS. 18837 Cpl. NUTTALL. H. 8th K.O.R.L.	
			9522 Pte. EDMONDSON G.G. 2nd SUFFOLKS. 19761 Pte. KENYON. A. do do	
			9154 Pte. LANKESTER. W. do do 20158 Pte. BATES. G. 4th R.FUS.	
			23123 Pte. MOORE. A. do do 13393 Pte. PERKINS. J. do do	
			18441 Pte SLINN. J. 7 Yks & LANCS. P.B	
			To ZUDAUSQUES. to 1R.S.F. re Pte. McCAFFERTY. J. Office routine	
	27.6.16		To HOULLE. Inspection of T.V. men by ADMS. Surplus stores sent to WATTEN. STA Office routine Pte. SLINN to WATTEN	
do	28.6.16		To ADMS & Q Office re Div. Move & detachment of lorry & men returned to units.	
			2 R.Scots 16968 PTE KELLY. A. 4 R.FUS. 13939 PTE MELLISH. A.	
			4 R.FUS. 21122 KINGSTON W. 6796 MIZON. W.	
			NCO's given freedom except Black. recalled to TILQUES. Office routine	

WAR DIARY or INTELLIGENCE SUMMARY

O.C. SA Sanitary Section Army Form C. 2118.
3D Division.

(Erase heading not required.)

Place	Date	Hour	Summary of Events and Information	Remarks and references to Appendices
TILQUES	29.6.16		The f/m P.B. men despatched to 2nd Army H.Q. CASSEL.	
			2 Roy. Scots. 4012 Pte. BROWN. T. 2 Roy. Scots. 8570 Pte. WILKES. E.J.	
			— — 4281 " DENVIR. E. Rl. Anglesey Eg. 6166 Spr. MARRION. E.	
			— — 13864 " TAGVE. J. 2 Suffolk. 9156 Pte KNIGHTS. F.	
			12 West Yks. 12407 Pte. BROWN. D.	
			To ADMS + O.C. Salvage Coy. Standing by for Div. move. Three emblem S/M.	
			To ADMS, Q Office, BAROS, O.C. Salvage Coy. Inspected Div. H.Q. S/M. sanitary office. Office routine.	
do.	30.6.16			

R.G. Matthews
Capt R.A.M.C.
O.C. Sanitary
3D Div.

August 1916

3rd Division

S 5 A. Sanitary Section

July 1916

COMMITTEE FOR THE
MEDICAL HISTORY OF THE
Date 13 SEP. 1916

3

WAR DIARY of O.C. 57 Sanitary Sectn. 3rd Division

Army Form C. 2118

INTELLIGENCE SUMMARY

(Erase heading not required.)

Hour, Date, Place	Summary of Events and Information	Remarks and references to Appendices
1/7/16 TILQUES	To Q offer ADMS. Marched to WIZERNES STATION. Entrained at 23.12. & proceeded to CANDAS. 8MN	
2/7/16 do	Arrived CANDAS 8 am. Marched from CANDAS STA. to LE MEILLARD. 8MN	
3/7/16 do	Left LE MEILLARD at 2am. Marched to BOURDON arriving midnight. Joined DAC group at BOURDON 8MN	
4/7/16 do	Under instructions from OC. DAC group left BOURDON 9pm. Marched to VIGNACOURT. At VIGNACOURT 3.30am we detached from DAC group & marched to FLESELLES en route for 9th Div. Arr. group. Arrived FLESELLES 7 am. 8MN	
5/7/16 do	Marched from FLESELLES to BERTANGLES where we see'sed qk Div 9th Dn train. Reported to 9th Dn HQ at POULAINVILLE. Marched from BERTANGLES to LA HOUSSOYE 8MN	

WAR DIARY

for 5A Sanitary Section, 3rd Division. Army Form C. 2118.

or

INTELLIGENCE SUMMARY.

(Erase heading not required.)

Instructions regarding War Diaries and Intelligence Summaries are contained in F.S. Regs., Part II. and the Staff Manual respectively. Title pages will be prepared in manuscript.

Hour, Date, Place	Summary of Events and Information	Remarks and references to Appendices
6/7/16 Field.	Marched from LA HOUSSOYE to CORBIE. Reported to ADMS.	
7/7/16 do	At CORBIE. Arranged baths for section. Inspection of helmet, goggles, gum return, feet. 8MM	
8/7/16 do	To ADMS. Marched from CORBIE to crossing of BRAY-CORBIE road & MORLANCOURT-CHIPILLY road. 8MM	
9/7/16 do	Two NCOs sent to Div H.Q. at SAPPER CORNER. 8MM	
10/7/16 do	Moved from to BRONFAY FARM. To ADMS. 8MM	
11/7/16 CARNOY	To CARNOY. Reconnoitred Railway to MONTAUBAN. Showered officer to transport & various officers of 27th – 28th F.A. To ADM. 8MM	
12/7/16 do	Marched to CARNOY. To dug outs in MONTAUBAN valley. 8MM Took NCos & men of section over line from CARNOY to BERNAFAY WOOD. 8MM	

WAR DIARY for SA Sanitary Section 3rd Division
or
INTELLIGENCE SUMMARY.

Army Form C. 2118.

Instructions regarding War Diaries and Intelligence Summaries are contained in F.S. Regs., Part II. and the Staff Manual respectively. Title pages will be prepared in manuscript.

(Erase heading not required.)

Hour, Date, Place	Summary of Events and Information	Remarks and references to Appendices
13/7/16 MONTAUBAN	Saw officer i/c lines — arranged for further supply of trucks specially for RAMC. Arranged for experimental trips for men of section — for transference of stretcher cases from 3rd Div. DSM railhead to dressing stations. Evacuating wounded all night. SJM	
14/7/16 do	Evacuating wounded from MONTAUBAN to CARNOY. SJM	
15/7/16 do	Evacuating wounded. Returned to BRONFAY FARM at night. SJM	
16/7/16 do	To ARMY. To CORBIE to 3rd Div Supply Column workshops to arrange for return of lorry. SJM	
17/7/16 BRONFAY FARM	Sanitary work at various BRONFAY FARM. To Q office taking SJM	
18/7/16 BRONFAY FARM	Took 4 NCO men to quarry between MONTAUBAN & LONGUEVAL for sanitary duties. To ARMY Q officer & gave details for sanitary work in CARNOY. SJM	

WAR DIARY
or
INTELLIGENCE SUMMARY.

(Erase heading not required.)

Army Form C. 2118.

F.O.E. Sanitary Section
3rd Division

Hour, Date, Place		Summary of Events and Information	Remarks and references to Appendices
19/7/16	BRONFAY FARM	Sanitary work in CARNOY + BRONFAY FARM area. Interviews with Mayor of CARNOY re ADWS	SWM
20/7/16	BRONFAY FARM	Sanitary work in CARNOY. To ADWS	SWM
21/7/16	do	Lorry returns from Supply Column workshops. Sanitary work in CARNOY & BRONFAY FARM area. To ADMS	SWM
22/7/16	do	Sanitary work in trenches around BRONFAY FARM	SWM
23/7/16	do	Sanitary work on Corps "B". To Q Office re ADWS	SWM
24/7/16	do	To CARNOY. Interviews with O.C. Salvage Coy Capt WILLS, 18th Hussars re sanitation [illegible] in LONGUEVAL. To A.D.M.S	SWM
25/7/16	do	Sanitary work at Corps "B". To ADWS Re both of FODEN THRESH disinfectors for use of mine. o.c. main mess sta.	SWM
26/7/16	do	To MEAULTE, VILLE, TREUX, MERICOURT with ADWS re baths for Division	SWM
27/7/16	field	Moved from BRONFAY FARM to TREUX. Foster Thresh disinfector removed from main Dressing Station	SWM

WAR DIARY
INTELLIGENCE SUMMARY

(Erase heading not required.)

Army Form C. 2118.

F.O.C. 57 Sanitary Section 31 Division

Hour, Date, Place	Summary of Events and Information	Remarks and references to Appendices
28/7/16 TREUX	To baths at VILLE-SUR-ANCRE. Purses to VILLE with fatigue. Fresh disinfector took over duties & horses took disinfector from 14th Division. JM	
29/7/16 VILLE	XVR Corps collected ground battalions left by 31st Division. To ADMS, O/ffice, CRE, +O.C. 56R Regt by MR. Calls paid by ADMS. Proving papers to BATHS. Numbers bathed 476. Disposing cleaning up & took over command. JM	
30/7/16 VILLE	To ADMS Office re collection washing of underclothing. To CRE re baths at MEAULTE. To BADOE NCO's details for inspection of camps in SR + 9R Bde. Numbers bathed 288. JM	
31/7/16 VILLE	To ADMS & CRE. Soiled underclothing collected by lorry (2000 articles) Inspected camp of 13 KINGS (1st Bn) Regt at VILLE. Subsequent visit to ADMS, APM, CRE, + 46th Bde. Numbers bathed 696. JM	

A.M. Mathews Capt. RAMC
O.C. San. Sec. 31 Div.

WAR DIARY

of

O.C. 5A SANITARY SECTION, 3RD DIVISION.

for the month of August, 1916.

G.W. Mathews
Capt. RAMC
O.C.

COMMITTEE FOR THE
MEDICAL HISTORY OF THE WAR
Date :- 5 OCT. 1916

WAR DIARY *A/C SA Sanitary Section* Army Form C. 2118.
3rd Division
INTELLIGENCE SUMMARY
(Erase heading not required.)

Hour, Date, Place	Summary of Events and Information	Remarks and references to Appendices
1/8/16 VILLE-SUR-ANCRE	To ADMS, DADOS, Q Office re pershing. To CRE +OC Salvage Coy. To staff capt. QMGBde re baths. Continue work at baths. Potable water disinfector found to be giving unsatisfactory results. To 20th KRRC re washing. Visit from M.O. ic 14th KRR +OC XV Corps water column to arrange baths. 2000 pieces sent to AMIENS for washing. Number bathed 521	SLW
2/8/16 VILLE.	To ADMS, CRE, APM, & YMCA. HQ at MERICOURT. To Q Office. Potable water disinfector returned by XV Corps. To ADMS + Q Office re baths for artillery units. Arranged with staff capt. 9th Bde for 4 fatigue men from 9th Bde to work at baths. To DADOS 2000 pieces sent to laundry. Number bathed 631	SLW
3/8/16 VILLE.	To AMIENS to laundry. Forden truck disinfector arrives from main Dressing Station. XIII Corps. Repair to shower bath completed. 2000 pieces to laundry. Numbers bathed 199	SLW

WAR DIARY or INTELLIGENCE SUMMARY

Army Form C. 2118.

of O.C. SA Sanitary Section, 3rd Division

Hour, Date, Place	Summary of Events and Information	Remarks and references to Appendices
4/8/16 VILLE	To ADMS. Thence under instructions from ADMS to MEAULTE. Inspected new bath house site with Staff Capt 8th Bde & advised re soakage pits. To 22nd, 40th & 42nd Bdes R.F.A. to arrange for baths. Fodenthirsh loaves 2000 pieces to laundry. Numbers bathed 635. Drew 5000 hr impar 8/M/M	
5/8/16 VILLE	To 9th Bde H.Q. 476th Field Coy R.E. To 42nd Bde R.F.A. Altering improving baths. Fodenthirsh visits baths visited by DADOS 8/M/M 2000 pieces to laundry. numbers bathed 707	
6/8/16 VILLE	To 40th & 42nd Bde HQ R.F.A. To CRE & 9th Bde H.Q. Interviewed Q.M. 4 R.F. re clothing. To DADOS. Fodenthirsh returned from 76th Bde. numbers bathed 684. 8/M/M	
7/8/16 VILLE	To DADOS 7PM. To 9th Bde H.Q. Inspected camps of 9th M.Gun Coy, 9th Bde H.Q. & 9th Bde T.mortar Battery. Pow men of section attached regimental fatigue. 2000 pieces to laundry. numbers bathed 939 8/M/M	

Army Form C. 2118.

WAR DIARY of OC Sanitary Section
or
INTELLIGENCE SUMMARY. 3rd Division.

(Erase heading not required.)

Instructions regarding War Diaries and Intelligence Summaries are contained in F.S. Regs, Part II. and the Staff Manual respectively. Title pages will be prepared in manuscript.

Hour, Date, Place	Summary of Events and Information	Remarks and references to Appendices
8/8/16 VILLE.	To ADMS & Q Office re payment for washing disinfector camp of 151st Bty RFA and mo to 76th Bde HQ MERICOURT to arrange for fatigue man for baths. To 8th Bde HQ MEAULTE. Visited baths at MEAULTE & prisoners officers RE i/c. 2000 pieces to laundry. Number baths 668. SWW	
9/8/16 VILLE.	To 8th Bde HQ MEAULTE. To OC IV Corps Water Column. Detailed NCOs for inspection of camps. Inspected section of 3 D.A.C. with m.o. Work at baths. 2000 pieces to laundry. Number baths 703. SWW	
10/8/16 VILLE	To A.P.M., DADOS & DADMS. Inspected YMCA hut in VILLE. To Iwin major VILLE & to 13th Kings to arrange for clearing up transport & rubbish at YMCA hut. Inspected camp of 13th Kings with m.o. 2000 pieces to laundry. Number baths 389. SWW	
11/8/16 VILLE.	To DADOS & Q Office. Inspected camps Army. IN7. To 9th Bde HQ & 41st Poly. To ADMS visit from Staff Capt 76th Bde. OC IV Corps Water Col. 2000 pieces to laundry. Number baths 916. SWW	

(73989) W4141—463. 400,000. 9/14. H.&J.Ltd. Forms/C. 2118/10.

WAR DIARY of the Sanitary Section 3rd Division.

or

INTELLIGENCE SUMMARY.

Army Form C. 2118.

(Erase heading not required.)

Hour, Date, Place	Summary of Events and Information	Remarks and references to Appendices
12/8/16 VILLE	Inspected batteries wagon lines of 23 & 40 & 128 Bde R.F.A. To Aining at FORKED TREE. 2000 pces to laundry. Number bottles 464	
13/8/16 VILLE	Interview with A.D.M.S. re storage of clothes. Pais laundry account - AMIENS. 2000 pces to laundry. No bottles 789	SMW
14/8/16 VILLE	To Ypres hut VILLE. Inspected sanitary arrangements. Inspected 42 Bde Battery lines R.F.A. 2000 pces to laundry. Number bottles 616	SMW
15/8/16 VILLE	Foden Trush disinfector despatches to Town Mayor HORLANCOURT with instructions. Armoring Handes on battles to 55th Division. Moved to Gt BEAR COPSE. Interview with A.D.V.S., Officer i/c roads 2000 pces to laundry	SMW
16/8/16 LITTLE BEAR COPSE	Moved to LITTLE BEAR COPSE. N.C.O. detailed for sanitary supervision at battle HQ. To proving yards. 2000 pces to laundry	SMW

WAR DIARY
or
INTELLIGENCE SUMMARY.

Army Form C. 2118.

of O.C. Sanitary Section 3rd Division

(Erase heading not required.)

Hour, Date, Place	Summary of Events and Information	Remarks and references to Appendices
17/8/16 LITTLE BEAR COPSE	To CARNOY & TALLUS BOIS EE. Interviews Staff Capt Strickland re Sanitation of valley. Inspected bath huts in CARNOY. also trenches in CARNOY valley. Section NCOs men engaged in sanitary work in valley. To Q office re payment by bath. at VILLE. NCOs detailed to supervise sanitation of Divl transport lines. 2000 piece to Laundry. S.M.M.	
18/8/16 do	To WEST PERONNE & BILLON WOOD to interview O.C. officers of 142 Famb. re shower baths in CARNOY. To A.D.M.S., D.A.D.O.S. & Q Office. To CARNOY. Inspected baths. H.Q. BILLON COPSE S.M.M	
19/8/16 do do	To A.D.M.S. Q. Office. D.A.D.O.S. & S.S.O. Inspected lines of 3rd D.A.C. with M.O. In accordance with instructions from A.D.M.S. marched to MEAULTE route over baths. S.M.M	
20/8/16 MEAULTE.	Work on baths & engine. Baths inspected by A.A. & Q.M.G. Visited A.D.M.S. & D.D.O. Arranged baths for Shrapnel with Staff Captain. S.M.M	

WAR DIARY of O.C. SA Sanitary Section Army Form C. 2118.
or
INTELLIGENCE SUMMARY.   3rd Division

(Erase heading not required.)

Instructions regarding War Diaries and Intelligence Summaries are contained in F.S. Regs., Part II. and the Staff Manual respectively. Title pages will be prepared in manuscript.

Hour, Date, Place	Summary of Events and Information	Remarks and references to Appendices
21/8/16 MEAULTE	To AMIENS. Paid laundry account to date + brought back all remaining underclothing. Bathes used by 5th Bde	
22/8/16 do	To DAOURS to arrange for disposal of underclothing at bath. Dirty underclothes later to MERICOURT to be sent to PARIS. 76th Bde used baths 8/hr	
23/8/16 Field	Marched to MERICOURT + entrained for CANDAS. Marched from there to BERNAVILLE 8/hr	
24/8/16 BERNAVILLE	At BERNAVILLE. Paid men of section. 8/hr	
25/8/16 Field	Marched to FROHEN-LE-GRAND 8/hr	
26/8/16 Field	Proceeded by motor bus with section to NOUEX-LES-MINES. Interviewed Town mayor + arranged to place Field Ambulance Baths, laundry 8/hr	

WAR DIARY of O.C. SA Sanitary Section 3rd Division

INTELLIGENCE SUMMARY
(Erase heading not required.)

Army Form C. 2118.

Instructions regarding War Diaries and Intelligence Summaries are contained in F.S. Regs., Part II. and the Staff Manual respectively. Title pages will be prepared in manuscript.

Hour, Date, Place	Summary of Events and Information	Remarks and references to Appendices
27/8/16. NOUEX-LES-MINES	Interviewed Town Major, ADMS 40th Div, OC. 137 F.A. + OC Laundry 16th Division. 8hrs	
28/8/16. NOUEX.	Places holding parties at Field Ambulances, baths, + laundry. Interviewed Town Major re: Qing. fetches clothing from laundry. Arranges to clear baths. 8hrs	
29/8/16. NOUEX	To MAZINGARBE. Inspected baths. Interviewed Town Major Disinfector boiler in BRUAY. 8hrs	
30/8/16. NOUEX	Interviewed Town Major re Awning, & Area R.O.O. Arranges for testing of water supplies in NOUEX & MAZINGARBE. Sanitary work in NOUEX. 8hrs	
31/8/16. NOUEX.	To Town Major to arrange for fatigue men. To O offices, baths, ADMS General Sanitary work in NOUEX. 8hrs	Matthews Capt. RAMC O.C. Sanitary Sn. Div

Sept 1916

S No. 5a. Sanitary Section

3rd Divn

COMMITTEE FOR THE
MEDICAL HISTORY OF THE WAR
Date 26 OCT. 1916

SECRET

Vol 8

WAR DIARY.
OF

O.C. 5A SANITARY SECTION.

3RD DIVISION.

GMathews.
Capt RAMC
OC 5A Sander
3 Div

WAR DIARY of O.C. Sanitary Section Army Form C. 2118.
or
INTELLIGENCE SUMMARY. 3rd Division.

(Erase heading not required.)

Hour, Date, Place		Summary of Events and Information	Remarks and references to Appendices
NOEUX-LES-MINES	1/9/16	To O office re baths, laundry. 90 men reported for duty at the laundry from 8th & 10th Bdes. To O.C. Div. Supply Column re lorry for clothes, blankets into ADH8. SW/1	
do	2/9/16	To BETHUNE. Inspected laundry, arranged to start work. Interview with Town Mayor at MAZINGARBE re sanitary work in forward area. Inspected baths, sulphur ovens & brewery.	
do	3/9/16	Inspected general sanitary arrangements of NOUEX unit. ADH8. To MAZINGARBE to arrange for coal per pithead to baths. General sanitary work in NOUEX. SW/1	
do	4/9/16	To Town Mayor NOEUX. Arranged with O.Cs 142 & 1 Fd Amb to hand over baths at NOUEX MAZINGARBE. Drew 1500 fr in payment a/c Pois NCOs i/c of Section Sergeants A.B. & C. Made sanitary office of Div HQ SW/1	

Army Form C. 2118.

WAR DIARY of O.C. Sanitary Section
or
INTELLIGENCE SUMMARY. 3rd Division
(Erase heading not required.)

Instructions regarding War Diaries and Intelligence
Summaries are contained in F. S. Regs., Part II
and the Staff Manual respectively. Title pages
will be prepared in manuscript.

Hour, Date, Place	Summary of Events and Information	Remarks and references to Appendices
NOVEX LES MINES 5/9/16	To Town Major NOVEX and OC3 inlets latrines. Purchased antiseptic Sulphates with Bearing Stores & water supply. To OC No 7742 F.Amb - re baths. Interviews with OC Sanitar 8th Division. SMM	
do 6/9/16	To MAZINGARBE with Staving. Inspected baths & general sanitary arrangements. With in NOVEX. Interviews with DDMS Corps. SMM	
do 7/9/16	To Town Major NOVEX. 10 Office. Interviews NOVEX. Interviews with Army re methods to Arrange to have in charge of bath. laundry to h.o. to BW Train inspected Other places sharp. SMM	
do 8/9/16	To MAZINGARBE. Interviewed Town Major NOVEX General sanitary work in NOVEX. Inspects baths at NOVEX & Div laundry BETHUNE with h.o. h.o. BW Train. Inspects div. plans both. SMM	

(73989) W4141—463. 400,000. 9/14. H.&J.L&. Forms/C. 2118/10.

WAR DIARY of OC Sanitary Section Army Form C. 2118.
5th Division
INTELLIGENCE SUMMARY.
(Erase heading not required.)

Hour, Date, Place	Summary of Events and Information	Remarks and references to Appendices
9/9/16 NOEUX	To MAZINGARBE. Interviewed Town Major. Inspected baths with ADMS arrange is hand in charge to Town Major. NOEUX General Sanitary work continued. Conferred re sanitation.	
10/9/16 do	To OC Salvage Corps P.B. in our Inspected 8th Tn 67th Fld Transport Lines. Arranged for new latrines. Inspected latrines in NOEUX. Instructed manager for inspection of front water supplies for actg 6 Carpentier shops. To 8th Fde HQ	
11/9/16 do	To BETHUNE. Paid women employed in connection with Div. Laundry. Paid for baths at MAZINGARBE. Interviewed ADMS & OC Fd. Laundry.	
12/9/16 do	To Q office raising. Inspected new baths at HAZINGARBE with DADQG & OC Baths. Sanitary inspection of MAZINGARBE & PHILOSOPHE. Interviewed Town Major of MAZINGARBE re R.I.3. plan. Received Reports in water supply to trenches.	

Army Form C. 2118.

Instructions regarding War Diaries and Intelligence Summaries are contained in F.S. Regs., Part II. and the Staff Manual respectively. Title pages will be prepared in manuscript.

WAR DIARY
or
INTELLIGENCE SUMMARY.
(Erase heading not required.)

of OC 5th Sanitary Section
3rd Division

Hour, Date, Place	Summary of Events and Information	Remarks and references to Appendices
13/9/16 NOUEX	To ADMS office Inspected latrines &c in NOUEX Suburans with OR back — to MAZINGARBE. Inspected Camp of 7&8 M.W. to & billets in village. JMM	
14/9/16 do	To ADMS. Visits various & rubbish dumps included transport lines of Sigs, Art, RE, & TM Bat. To PHILOSOPHE & MAZINGARBE Manures. Town incin. NOUEX & MAZINGARBE & Field Engineer re D dinam. JMM	
15/9/16 do	To trenches. Inspected water supplies in 1st Inf alleys Salonica Hqs of in jnrs, Bkng & Infs. JMM	
16/9/16 do	To ADMS Inspected billets & sanitary arrangement at PHILOSOPHE & MAZINGARBE. JMM	
17/9/16 do	To CCS spring Sulcurans Tour Major NOUEX. Inspected huts at MAZINGARBE. Squad reentering work in NOUEX. JMM	

WAR DIARY of O.C. Sanitary Section 8th Division

INTELLIGENCE SUMMARY

Hour, Date, Place	Summary of Events and Information	Remarks and references to Appendices
18/9/16 NOUEX	To ARRAS, O.C. 8th Div H.Q. by car. Interviews Div. Drainage Officer, who went through to PHILOSOPHE. Interviews D.A.D.S. & R. Foulis. (OC Field San. Co. 23) Arranges for chlorination of water supply to trenches. SMM	
19/9/16 Do	To ARRAS, CRE. Interviews O.C. E. Riding Field Coy RE about chly water troughs? Inspected 8th Div. Sanitary Workshop at LAGORGUE SMM	
20/9/16 Do	To Armd Ques??? sanitary conference with DWS at VILLERS to CRE. SMM	
21/9/16	To MAZINGARBE & PHILOSOPHE. Inspects hutments & billets. To ARRAS H.Q. Drew Norfolk destructor. Inspection by DWS. SMM	

WAR DIARY of O.C. 5ᴬ Sanitary Sectⁿ Army Form C. 2118
3ᴅ Division

INTELLIGENCE SUMMARY
(Erase heading not required.)

Hour, Date, Place	Summary of Events and Information	Remarks and references to Appendices
22/9/16 NOUEX.	Arrangements for move. Inspected billets. Sanitary arrangements in NOUEX-LE-MINES. Interviewed Town Mayor about CRE. To 76th Bde. HQ. re move. SHM	
23/9/16 Field	Marched with 76th Bde group to ALLOUAGNE. SHM	
24/9/16 Field	Moved to SERNY Heure to Div. HQ at BOMY'S SHM	
25/9/16 BOMY.	To ADMS Distributed NCOs of section over Div. area. Interview with O.C. Batts. SHM	
26/9/16 BOMY.	Inspected Div. HQ. Sanitary arrangements & water supplies. Interviewed SSO. Arranges latrines for HQ. SHM	
27/9/16 do	To COYECQUES. Interviewed M.O. of 2 Royal Scots. re water supply, sanitation of battalion area. Interviews MO. 1R.Scots Fus. at DENNEBROUECQ. re water supply. To ADMS SHM	

WAR DIARY of O.C. 57 Sanitary Section — Army Form C. 2118
or
INTELLIGENCE SUMMARY. 3rd Division
(Erase heading not required.)

Hour, Date, Place	Summary of Events and Information	Remarks and references to Appendices
28/9/16 BOMY	Inspected billets of New York Regt at PETTIGNY with M.O. Interviewed M.O. of 7 King's SHROPSHIRE L.I. at RECLINGHEM. Inspected water supply at GRUEPPE. S/M	
29/9/16 do	General sanitary routine work. Interviewed M.O. of 18 Kings (L'pool) Regt & 2 SUFFOLKS & inspected water supplies in ERNY ST JULIEN & ENQUIN-LES-MINES. Interviews with O.C. Batt. & O.C. office. S/M	
30/9/16 do	Interviewed M.O. 8 NORKS at DELETTE & inspected water supplies. Inspected water supplies of 2 R.SCOTS & 1 R.SCOTS FUS in COYECQUES & DENNEB ROUSCQ. Paid men of section. Inspected gas helmets & non-returns. S/M
J.M Matthews S/M
Capt R.A.M.C
O.C 57 San Sec
3rd Div	

Oct 1916

3rd Division 140/1128

S

5th Sanitary Section

Cct 1916

COMMITTEE FOR THE
MEDICAL HISTORY OF THE WAR
Date -2 DEC. 1916

Vol 9

War Diary.
of
O.C. 5A Sanitary Section
For
October 1916.

R. Matthews
Captain,
OC.

WAR DIARY or INTELLIGENCE SUMMARY.

Army Form C. 2118

of O.C. 5ᴬ Sanitary Section 38ᵗʰ Division

(Erase heading not required.)

Instructions regarding War Diaries and Intelligence Summaries are contained in F.S. Regs., Part II. and the Staff Manual respectively. Title pages will be prepared in manuscript.

Hour, Date, Place	Summary of Events and Information	Remarks and references to Appendices
1/10/16. BOMY.	Interviewed M.O. of 1 N. Fus. at BEAUMETZ-LES-AIRES & inspected billets & water supply. Inspected water supply of 4 Roy. Fus. at LAIRE with M.O. to hand. 8hrs	
2/10/16 do	To 10 R. WELCH FUS at LETTRES. Interviewed M.O. inspected billets & water supply. Inspected billets of 1 GORDON. HRS at ESTREE BLANCHE with M.O. Interviewed Staff Capt. 76th Bde. inspected Bde.H.Q. Arrange to disinfect billets of 10 R.W.F. 8hrs	
3/10/16 do	Interviewed M.O. 8K.O.Roy Lancs. inspected water supply. Inspected water supply 142 F.AMB. at CUHEM also supply at GRUEPPE & 9K Bde M.Gun Cy billets. 8hrs	
4/10/16 do	Preparation for Div. Move 8hrs	
5/10/16 do	Marched to MONCHY - CAYEUX. 8hrs	
6/10/16 do	At MONCHY - CAYEUX. ~~8hrs~~	
7/10/16 do	Marched to ST POL. Entrained for ACHEUX 8hrs	

WAR DIARY
or
INTELLIGENCE SUMMARY.

Army Form C. 2118

of O.C. 50 Sanitary Section 31 Division

(Erase heading not required.)

Hour, Date, Place	Summary of Events and Information	Remarks and references to Appendices
7/10/16 Field	Returned at PUCHEVILLERS. Marched to BERTRANCOURT. SMM	
8/10/16 BERTRANCOURT	Interviewed A/Tn/ Town Major. Inspected water supplies & camps in village. Interviewed M.O. 11 W.Yorks. SMM	
9/10/16 do	To Town Major. Inspected RCRL camp with M.O. Interviewed M.O. 8 Suffolks, is using hyp't inspected camps. SMM	
10/10/16 do	Inspected water supplies in BUS. Interviewed Town Major of BEAUSSART. Gen'l note made re H.Q. camp in BERTRANCOURT. SMM	
11/10/16 do	Interviewed Staff Capt. 76 Bde. Inspected Camp of 10 R.W.F. with M.O. Arranges for water supply at Bus for elimination of BERTRANCOURT supply. Drew 1500 g. from field cashier. SMM	
12/10/16 do	Inspected camp of 10 R.W. Fusiliers with M.O. & billets in town. Inspected 76 Bde H.Q. Cny. & T. Munster Btty. billets also 76 Bde H.Q. Inspected camp of 2 Suffolks with M.O. SMM	

WAR DIARY of O.C. 5? Sanitary Section Army Form C. 2118
3rd Division

INTELLIGENCE SUMMARY.
(Erase heading not required.)

Hour, Date, Place	Summary of Events and Information	Remarks and references to Appendices
13/10/16 BERTRANCOURT.	To MAILLY WOOD. Inspected camps of 13 King L' post, 4 King Shrop.L.I. + K. Yorks with M.O.'s i/c. SMM	
14/10/16 do	To Kendies with ADMS Inspected transport camps of 76th-able units. SMM	
15/10/16 do	To ACHEUX Inspected camps of 2 R. Scots. 1st Gordn H. with M.O.'s. Paid visit of section Inspected transport camps of units of 8th 9th Bdes. SMM	
16/10/16 do	Inspected bath supplies at BUS + ACHEUX Interviewed O.C. water patrol. Inspected camp of Suffolks with M.O. SMM	
17/10/16 do	Interviewed camp commandant MAILLY WOOD re sanitation of Camps. Also Town Major BEAUSSART. Interviewed O.C. sange. 51st Div at BUS. SMM	
18/10/16 Ref.	Arms with Bn. H.Q. 5 BUS-LES-ARTOIS. SMM	
19/10/16 BUS-LES-ARTOIS	To ADMS Town Major water supplies in BUS Later to LOUVENCOURT. Interviewed Town Major arranged for camp sanitation. SMM	

WAR DIARY of O.C. 50 Sanitary Section 3D Division

INTELLIGENCE SUMMARY

Place	Date	Hour	Summary of Events and Information	Remarks and references to Appendices
Bus-les-Artois	24/10/16		To LOUVENCOURT. Interviewed Town Major. Arranged matter of putrescine. Inspected C.R.A., other H.Q. billets in Bus.	
do	23/10/16		Clayton Sulphur Disinfector erected in 142 F.A. Arranged with O.C. Adv. Workshops to repair. Inspected sundry detail camps at COURCELLES.	SMM
do	22/10/16		Inspected water supplies at LOUVENCOURT. Interviewed Staff Capt. 9th Bde. & inspected Bde. H.Q. Received reports re units sanit. rubbish. Bus supplies.	SMM
do	23/10/16		Inspected camps of S.E. YORKS & 1 R. SCOTS FUS with M.O.S. Interviewed M.O. etc. 10 R. WELSH FUS. & Inspected some billets. To A.D.M.S.	SMM
do	24/10/16		To ORVILLE to disinfect billets of 5 Corps mounted troops. Funeral with Clayton disinfector. Sacks after repair. Received sundry sanitary reports.	SMM
do	26/10/16		Inspected brigade transport lines & artillery camps. Blankets disinfected.	SMM
do	27/10/16		To COURCELLES. Inspected billets of Suffolk Regt. with M.O. Inspected billets in Bus - interviewed Town Major.	SMM

WAR DIARY
or
INTELLIGENCE SUMMARY.

Army Form C. 2118.

of O.C. San Sanitary Section 3rd Division

(Erase heading not required.)

Place	Date	Hour	Summary of Events and Information	Remarks and references to Appendices
Dus ES ARRAS	28/10/16		To LOUVENCOURT. Inspected camps & billets of B. Kings (L'pool) Regt. Interviewed Town Major. Inspected water supplies. Shm	
do	29/10/16		To LOUVENCOURT. Inspected billets of 12 W. Yorks & 1 N. Fus. Sanitary report Shm 15 ADMS. Saw men of section.	
do	30/10/16		To VAUCHELLES. Inspected camp of 4 R. Fus & 2 R. Scots. Interviewed no 2 4 R. Fus. Received Sunday sanitary water cart reports. Shm	
do	31/10/16		To COURCELLES. Interviewed Town Major inspected camp billets with him. Inspected camp & S.H.O. Royal Fus. & billets of 10 R.W. Fus with Shm	

AMMathews
Capt RAMC

DCSoSomber
3rd Div.

Nov. 1916
3rd Div.
md/1846
Confidential
No. 10

WAR DIARY OF

O.C. 5th SANITARY SECTION, 3rd DIV.

FOR

NOVEMBER 1916.

COMMITTEE FOR THE
MEDICAL HISTORY OF THE WAR
Date -3 JAN. 1917

WAR DIARY or INTELLIGENCE SUMMARY.
Army Form C.2118.

of O.C. Sanitary Section 3rd Division

(Erase heading not required.)

Instructions regarding War Diaries and Intelligence Summaries are contained in F. S. Regs., Part II. and the Staff Manual respectively. Title pages will be prepared in manuscript.

Place	Date	Hour	Summary of Events and Information	Remarks and references to Appendices
Bus.	1/4/16		To Louvencourt. Interviewed Town Major. Inspected water supply. Inspected billets of F.W. Fus. To Acheux.	B.W. Shm
do	2/4/16		Inspected camps of 2 Suffolks + 1 Gordons in Bus Wood. Inspected transport lines of 8th Bde.	Shm
do	3/4/16		To Courcelles. Interviewed Town Major. Inspected billets of 2 R. Scots. N.C.O. details for work in Courcelles. Work with Clayton disinfector.	Shm
do	4/4/16		Inspected 76th Inf Bde Cy Camp. Interviewed C.O. Inspected Brit. Hq. Interviewed Town Major of Bus.	Shm
do	5/4/16		To 76th Inf Gun Cy Camp. Inspected. 3rd Div Sig. Cy camp. Eden Thresh disinfector returned for duty with division. Arrived.	Shm
do	6/4/16		To Vauchelles. Inspected camps of 4 R. Fus. + 2 R. Scots. Visit from O.C. Sansee 2nd Div.	Shm
do	7/4/16		To Courcelles. Inspected billets of 12 W.Yorks + N. Fus. Work with disinfector. To O.C. Adv. workshops unit.	Shm
do	8/4/16		Inspected billets & camps with A.D.M.S. + A.A.Q.M.G. To Town Major Bus. Arranges fatigue party from 1 GRNF.	Shm

1577 Wt.W10791/1773 500,000 1/15 D. D. & L. A.D.S.S./Forms/C. 2118.

WAR DIARY of O.C. 50 Sanitary Section — 2nd Division

INTELLIGENCE SUMMARY

Place	Date	Hour	Summary of Events and Information	Remarks and references to Appendices
Bus	9/4/16		To COLINCAMPS + EUSTON DUMP with AD.M.S. Work with disinfector taking Samples.	SMW
do	10/4/16		Inspection of THRESH + CLAYTON disinfectors by A.D.M.S. To M.O. of 10 R. WELSH Fus. Inspected billets of 10 R.W.F. To LOUVENCOURT. Selected site for public latrines. Inspected camp of R. SCOTS Fus.	SMW
do	11/4/16		Conference at A.D.M.S. office. Inspected various billets. M.O.'s interviewed. Town Major.	SMW
do	12/4/16		Recalled publication from LOUVENCOURT. Proceeded with section to trenches.	SMW
do	13/4/16		Section sketches leaving from OBSERVATION WOOD + FLAG 8 AVENUE to EUSTON DUMP.	SMW
do	14/4/16		Sketches leaving, marches back to Bus at night.	SMW
do	15/4/16		Subsection despatched to LOUVENCOURT + N.C.O.'s to Bde H.Q.	SMW
do	16/4/16		To LOUVENCOURT. Interviewed sanitary adviser to Town Major. To dump.	SMW
do	17/4/16		Inspected camps in BUS WOOD + billets of 1 N. Fusiliers, also camp of + R.F.'s in Bus. Inspected detail camp.	SMW

WAR DIARY of O.C. 50 Sanitary Section Army Form C. 2118
or
INTELLIGENCE SUMMARY
(Erase heading not required.)

Instructions regarding War Diaries and Intelligence Summaries are contained in F.S. Regs., Part II. and the Staff Manual respectively. Title pages will be prepared in manuscript.

3rd Division

Place	Date	Hour	Summary of Events and Information	Remarks and references to Appendices
B.U.C.	18/4/16		Tests made in water carts for chlorination. To Town Major Bus. Sanitary report to ADMS	
do	19/4/16		Testing water in carts. Inspected some Brigade transport lines. Inspected camp of 8th Bn (L. Pool) Regt references no.	S.H.H
do	20/4/16		Conference at ADMS office. With no detail camp + billets under	S.H.H
do	21/4/16		Inspected baths in Bus Wood. To ADMS To Louvencourt. Returned from Major inspects billets camp & fatigue party. Went for walk	S.H.H
do	22/4/16		To Courcelles. Inspected billets camps & area with Town Major.	S.H.H
do	23/4/16		Inspected sunday billet in Bus. To ADMS. Sanitary Report + recommendations re Courcelles. Inspected billets of Forward Hughes. Inspected camp of Fonquevillers 8th 6th + 7th Res.	S.H.H
do	24/4/16		Tested chlorination of water carts. Walk in billets & camp meussilm.	S.H.H
do	25/4/16		Inspected billets camp + mess with DMS re arranges inspect parties	S.H.H
do	26/4/16		from W/RWF. Inspected billets of 49 Div KRR + KSLI + DK Regts with major to Town Major Bus & to Louvencourt. Reference Town Major	S.H.H

WAR DIARY of O.C. Sanitary Section 3rd Division

or

INTELLIGENCE SUMMARY.

(Erase heading not required.)

Army Form C. 2118

Instructions regarding War Diaries and Intelligence Summaries are contained in F. S. Regs., Part II. and the Staff Manual respectively. Title pages will be prepared in manuscript.

Place	Date	Hour	Summary of Events and Information	Remarks and references to Appendices
Bus	27/4/16		To COURCELLES. Interviewed Town Mayor there re U.R.R.C. Arranged with Greg for material for latrines. Report on watercarts to A.D.M.S. SW.	
do	28/4/16		Inspection of billets in COURCELLES with A.D.M.S. Interviewed O.C. 2/U.R.R.C. re Sanitation of COURCELLES. Visit from no 4 S. Yds. Pass work of section. SW	
do	29/4/16		Inspected Camp of 1st Regt. & detail camp in Bus. Material despatches to COURCELLES for latrines. Public latrine completed in Bus. To VAUCHELLES. Inspected billets of 1N. Fus + camp of 12 Wynds. SW	
do	30/4/16		To COURCELLES. re construction of public latrine. Inspected camp of 128T. with two interviews No. 6 S. Yds. Re. trestles. Tested water in watercarts for chlorination. SW	

[Signatures:]
C Matthews
Capt RAMC
O.C. Sanitary Sec.

[Stamp: 5P SANITARY SECTION 3rd DIVISION 17/5/16]

SECRET 3rd Pen 14/9/10 Vol XI

S¹ War Diary
5ᵃ Sanitary Section
from Dec 16 to 31 Dec 16

Dec 1916

COMMITTEE FOR THE
MEDICAL HISTORY OF THE WAR
Date 31 JAN. 1917

WAR DIARY of O.C. Sanitary Section 3rd Division

INTELLIGENCE SUMMARY

(Erase heading not required.)

Place	Date	Hour	Summary of Events and Information	Remarks and references to Appendices
Bus	1/3/16		To COURCELLES re construction of public latrines. Testing water in cart	Shm
do	2/3/16		Inspected billets in Bus. Sanitary report & reports on water carts to A.D.M.S	Shm Shm
do	3/3/16		To Henencourt. Inspected trenches in right sector. Inspected detail mens camp &c in Colmien	Shm
do	4/3/16		Bus. To Town Major Bus. To LOUVENCOURT Inspected post & billets scavenges by 3rd Div. To COURCELLES re Latrines. Took over duties S.O.C. Baths Laundry	Shm
do	5/3/16		To AMIENS to buy balls for Laundry roller, washing	Shm
do	6/3/16		Lectures to XIII Corps Cavalry at ORVILLE	Shm
do	7/3/16		Inspected billets of Suffolks. Received water cart reports. Issued anti-fly	Shm
do	8/3/16		in connection with baths	Shm
do	9/3/16		Inspected billets & camps in COURCELLES with A.D.M.S	Shm
do	10/3/16		To LOUVENCOURT Interviewed Town Major. Inspected billets & R.W. Fus. Report to 'Q' Office on baths sanitary & water cart reports leaving Shm	Shm
			Inspected billets of 8th R.Fus, R.Flying Corps. Detail camp Sunday Flew billets in 15th.	Shm

WAR DIARY of O.C. Sy Sanitary Section 3rd Division

INTELLIGENCE SUMMARY.

Place	Date	Hour	Summary of Events and Information	Remarks and references to Appendices
BUS	11.12.16		To Q Office re sewal work in connection with Latrines. To COURCELLES re Latrines. Inspected sundry billets with Town Mayor.	
do	12.12.16		To AMIENS to pay laundry bills.	
do	13.12.16		Conference at D.D.M.S. Office ACHEUX. Several sanitary work in Bus. Inspected billets in Bus.	
do	14.12.16		To COURCELLES, inspected water supply & billets.	
do	15.12.16		Inspected 9th Hrs fm Cy Camp 10th Div Stores in Bus Wood. New camp. Transport lines to Adjug. & Q. office.	
do	16.12.16		Conference at Army H.Q. To Army Sanitary water Reports	
do	17.12.16		Inspected billets & camps in Bus & COURCELLES with ADMS.	
do	18.12.16		To C.R.E. at Lebrens. Inspected new field billets in LOUVENCOURT. Returned had the R.W. Survey investigated water supply in COURCELLES.	
do	19.12.16		To C.R.E. Inspected camps of 45th & 29th Battns. New 500 yards from fields ashur ACHEUX. To COURCELLES fuires mens huts. Inspected latrines Report to ADMS on work from Bus Wood. Inspected new camp Arbuition- camp.	
do	20.12.16			

WAR DIARY

of O.C. 5A Sanitary Section, 3rd Division

Army Form C.2118.

INTELLIGENCE SUMMARY

(Erase heading not required.)

Place	Date	Hour	Summary of Events and Information	Remarks and references to Appendices
B v S	28.12.16		Handed my duties to M.O. ½ Train - Proceeded on leave 8am	
do	22.12.16		Routine work	
do	23.12.16		do	
do	24.12.16		do	
do	25.12.16		do	
do	26.12.16		do	
do	27.12.16		do	
do	28.12.16		do	
do	29.12.16		do	
do	30.12.16		do	
do	31.12.16		do	

Mathews
Capt RAMC
O.C.

5A SANITARY SECTION.
No. 3.1.17

140/94 Vol 12

3rd Answer.

Jan 1914

War Diary of No. 3rd Sanitary Section

May 1917

COMMITTEE FOR THE
MEDICAL HISTORY OF THE WAR
Date 13 MAR. 1917

WAR DIARY of O.C. 5ª Sanitary Section

Army Form C. 2118.

INTELLIGENCE SUMMARY

(Erase heading not required.)

Instructions regarding War Diaries and Intelligence Summaries are contained in F.S. Regs., Part II. and the Staff Manual respectively. Title pages will be prepared in manuscript.

Place	Date	Hour	Summary of Events and Information	Remarks and references to Appendices
Bus	1-1-17		Routine work BfS	
do	2-1-17		Routine work BfS	
do	3-1-17		To ADMS. on return from leave. Inspected R.A. camp & sundry billets in Bus.	Offr
do	4-1-17.		Inspected new camp & southern billets in Bus. To COURCELLES. Interviewed Town Major & received report of work done	Offr
do	5-1-17		Interviewed Town Major Bus. Inspected incinerant camp of infantry brigades & northern billets Bus.	Offr
do	6-1-17		To LOUVENCOURT. Inspected billets, latrines. Sanitary work.	Offr
do	7-1-17		General Sanitary work in connection with Divisional minor.	Offr
do	8-1-17		General sanitary work. Inspected camps in Bus wood & billets in Bus. Also transport camp & new infantry camp.	Offr
do	9-1-17		To ADMS 32ⁿᵈ Div. Inspected camp of 5-6ᵗʰ R Scots. Interviewed his Arranged for men of these Brumfutrs to LOUVENCOURT	Offr

A 5834 Wt. W 4973/M 687 750,000 8/16 D. D. & I. Ltd. Forms/C.2113/13.

WAR DIARY of O.C. SA Sanitary Section

Army Form C. 2118.

B.E.F.

INTELLIGENCE SUMMARY

Place	Date	Hour	Summary of Events and Information	Remarks and references to Appendices
Bus	10.1.17		To Army. Inspected Div. HQ. Interviewed Interviewed CRE re material & no. to train re supervision of Bus. men to 15th June Jnr. inspects camp	Shm
do	11.1.17		Inspected No 46 P. of war camp. To Q. Office Interviewed arranging General Sanitary work.	Shm
do	12.1.17		Inspected billets & camps in Bus with DADMS 3rd Div. Lt. McCar.C.Cashens RAMC attached for instructional purposes	Shm
do	13.1.17		Inspected "transport" camp at Bus & allotted site for permanent latrines. Commences running of well in Bus with Turn Major. Conference with DADMS at ACHEUX. Sanitary & water reports rendered	Shm
do	14.1.17		Inspected latrines, majority of billets in COURCELLES. Paid was N.C.Os. men of section. To Acheux & Turn Major Bus Thomas for permanent K work in COURCELLES. Early ayles	Shm
,,	15.1.17		Inspected cookhouses & sites in "transport" camp. Inspected infantry camp at Bus wood. To C.R.E. Acheux. Inspected Bus HQ. with Camp commandants	Shm
do	16.1.17		Inspected latrines & billets & threw Bonfeulie in LOUVENCOURT. Inspected water supplies, Reservoirs with Bus. Drew 250 fr in banknotes of	Shm

WAR DIARY for Sanitary Section

Army Form C. 2118.

INTELLIGENCE SUMMARY
(Erase heading not required.)

Place	Date	Hour	Summary of Events and Information	Remarks and references to Appendices
Bus	14.1.17		Inspected billets in Bus & Mausoir? camp. Drew camp re chlorination scheme for chlorine water. Inspected R.A. camps.	SM
do	16.1.17		Tests water in wells. Received reports on wells. Conference with DDMS at 5 Corps H.Q. Wells started in Mausoir? camp. Found latrines in Bus.	SM
do	19.1.17		Inspected Bourcelles & latrines. Reported to Issues from hypo ASC camps of 3rd Div. Tests water in various carts.	SM
do	20.1.17		Inspected camps of No.1 & No.4 Sections 32nd Div. Chose new site for manure dumps in Bus. To CRA re removal of manure & town works to repair. Sanitary & water reports to ADMS. Party of PR.	SM
do	21.1.17		With Town Major to inspect sites for manure dumps. To Euston Dump & Sucrerie to test water supply in trenches. Report to ADMS	SM

A5834 Wt. W4973/M687 750,000 8/16 D.D. & L. Ltd. Forms/C.2113/13.

Army Form C. 2118.

WAR DIARY
or
INTELLIGENCE SUMMARY.

of O.C. 54 Sanitary Section

(Erase heading not required.)

Instructions regarding War Diaries and Intelligence Summaries are contained in F. S. Regs., Part II. and the Staff Manual respectively. Title pages will be prepared in manuscript.

Place	Date	Hour	Summary of Events and Information	Remarks and references to Appendices
Bus	22.1.17		To Achiet. Move of 3rd Division to adjoining area. Billets in Bus occupied by Infantry, artillery & D.A.C. Camps. Inspected THIEVRES with Town Major & rendered report.	8km
do	23.1.17		To Achiet 62nd Division. Interview with O.C. San Sec 62nd Division. Inspected water supplies. To DDMS V Corps	8km
do	24.1.17		Arranged for policing front water column - arrg to forming of Standpipes & supplies from water column up to Town Major Bus. To Achiet 3rd Div re arr 62nd Div. Fatigue parties for work in Bus. Sanitary report to Town Major Bus.	8km
do	25.1.17		To Town Major re water supply. To COURCELLES. Interviewed Town Major & inspected some billets. To GUIGNEUX re manure dump for artillery	8km
do	26.1.17		To ORVILLE Inspected village with Town Major	8km

A.5834 Wt. W.4973/M687 750,000 8/16 D.D. & L. Ltd. Forms/C.2118/13.

WAR DIARY of O.C. S/Sanitary Section — Army Form C. 2118.

or

INTELLIGENCE SUMMARY.

(Erase heading not required.)

Place	Date	Hour	Summary of Events and Information	Remarks and references to Appendices
BUS	27/1/17		Interviews Town Mayor re sanitation of BUS. To JOUVENCOURT. Interviews Town Mayor inspects billets & camp. Sanitary reports. Visit from D.A.D.M.S. (sanitation) IV Army.	
do	28/1/17		Handed over to 62nd Div. San. Sec. Moved to CANAPLES	8 mm
FIELD	29/1/17		Moved from CANAPLES to FLERS	8 mm
do	30/1/17		Moved from FLERS to VILLERS CHATEL	8 mm
VILLERS CHATEL	31/1/17		Sanitary work in village	8 mm

R.P. Matthews
Capt. RAMC
O.C. S/Sanitary Section

3rd Vol.

WAR DIARY OF
O.C. 5A SANITARY SECTION
FOR
FEBRUARY 1917

COMMITTEE FOR THE
MEDICAL HISTORY OF THE WAR
Date 4= APR.1917

Army Form C. 2118.

WAR DIARY of J.C.B. 5th Sanitary Section
or
INTELLIGENCE SUMMARY.

(Erase heading not required.)

Instructions regarding War Diaries and Intelligence Summaries are contained in F.S. Regs., Part II. and the Staff Manual respectively. Title pages will be prepared in manuscript.

Place	Date	Hour	Summary of Events and Information	Remarks and references to Appendices
VILLERS-CHATEL	1.2.17		At VILLERS-CHATEL. Sanitary work in village. JMM.	
do	2.2.17		At VILLERS-CHATEL. JMM	
do	3.2.17		To AMBRINES. Inspected 76th Bde HQ & billets of 1 gordon High.	
do	4.2.17		To FREVILLERS. Inspected 9th RSF & H.Q. JMM	
do	5.2.17		At VILLERS-CHATEL JMM	
do	6.2.17		At VILLERS-CHATEL JMM	
do	7.2.17		At VILLERS-CHATEL	
do	8.2.17		Moved from VILLERS-CHATEL to LIGNEREUIL. Form flesh Brainfield S323 reported for duty	JMM
LIGNEREUIL	9.2.17		At LIGNEREUIL. Inspected village with Town Major. Brainfield returned to report to base. JMM	
do	10.2.17		Inspected 91st Bde HQ at HOUVIN-HOUVIGNEUIL JMM	
do	11.2.17		Moved from LIGNEREUIL to VAN QUETIN JMM	

Army Form C. 2118.

WAR DIARY of O.C. SA Sanitary Section
or
INTELLIGENCE SUMMARY.
(Erase heading not required.)

Instructions regarding War Diaries and Intelligence Summaries are contained in F. S. Regs., Part II. and the Staff Manual respectively. Title pages will be prepared in manuscript.

Place	Date	Hour	Summary of Events and Information	Remarks and references to Appendices
WAN QUETIN	12.2.17		Maurieus Town Major WAN QUETIN re sanitation. To WARLUS. Inspected Sn H.Q. & interviewed ADMS	SMN
do	13.2.17		Todes thresh Nomes for duty. Made tour of 8, 9, & 76th Bde area & San. Only area	SMN
do	14.2.17		Arranged distribution of looms N.Co's in Div. area. To WARLUS to ADMS	SMN
do	15.2.17		Inspected WAN QUETIN with Town Major. To ADMS	SMN
do	16.2.17		To HAUTEVILLE. Inspected village & camps. To WARLUS RDN HQ	SMN
do	17.2.17		Sanitary work in WAN QUETIN. To BEAUFORT. Inspected village	SMN
do	18.2.17		Conference at ADMS with O.C. 7 F.Amb. Sanitary reports to ADMS	SMN

A.5834 Wt. W4973/M687 750,000 8/16 D. D. & L. Ltd. Forms/C.2118/13.

Army Form C. 2118.

WAR DIARY of O.C.'s A Sanitary Section
INTELLIGENCE SUMMARY.
(Erase heading not required.)

Place	Date	Hour	Summary of Events and Information	Remarks and references to Appendices
WANQUETIN	19/1/17		To O.C. 14 Div Sanitary Section re sanitation in area. Took over sanitation of WARLUS. SMM	
do	20/1/17		To ARRAS with ADMS. SMM	
do	21/1/17		To ARRAS to put latrines for dressing station SMM	
do	22/1/17		Inspected WARLUS. To AVESNES. To NOYELLE VION Interviewed Camp Commandant VI Corps re Clayton Sulphur Disinfector arranges for use of same. To ETREE WAMIN Interviewed Town Major. SMM	
do	23/1/17		Inspected ETREE WAMIN with Town Major. To BERLENCOURT Inspected water supply with Town Major. To DOHS at NOYELLE VION. SMM	
do	24/1/17		To WARLUS. Interviewed Camp Comdt So Divion. Town Major & OC 14 Div Sanfer. To HAUTEVILLE Interviewed no 1/c R York & OC Hunballe Field Ambulance Drew 500h on inspect. To LIENCOURT Interviewed Town Major SMM N.C.O sent to VI Corps HQ.	

Army Form C. 2118.

WAR DIARY of 9 SA Sanitary Section

INTELLIGENCE SUMMARY.

(Erase heading not required.)

Place	Date	Hour	Summary of Events and Information	Remarks and references to Appendices
WANQUETIN	25/6/17		Sanitary reports on ETREE WAMIN, WARLUS to Arras & water cart report to ARRAS. Inspected billets of 2 Suffolk Regt with M.O. Pass NCO's & men of the section.	8am
do	26/6/17		To HAUTEVILLE. Inspected village, interviewed adjutant Br. 4pm re disinfection of blankets. To WARLUS. To Town Major ARRAS	8am
do	27/6/17		Work in WANQUETIN. Inspected various billets. Transfer to WARLUS 15 A.P.M. re traffic restriction. To S.S.O. re fuel.	8am
do	28/6/17		Moved to WARLUS.	8am

C.H. Matthews
Capt RAMC
O.C. 9 San Sec.

SANITARY SECTION
No. 13
Date 1/7/17
3rd DIVISION

140/2043

3rd Div (?)

No. 5a. Sanitary Section

Mar. 1917

COMMITTEE FOR THE
MEDICAL HISTORY OF THE WAR
Date 11 MAY 1917

Army Form C. 2118.

WAR DIARY
or
INTELLIGENCE SUMMARY.
(Erase heading not required.)

WAR DIARY OF
O.C. 5A SANITARY SECTION
FOR
MARCH 1917

Vol 14

J.P. Matthews
Capt RAMC
O/C Sa San Sec

WAR DIARY of O.C. Sanitary Section

INTELLIGENCE SUMMARY

Army Form C. 2118.

Place	Date	Hour	Summary of Events and Information	Remarks and references to Appendices
WARLUS	1/3/17		Work in WARLUS. To LIENCOURT re timber & carpenters for ETREE WAMIN. To BERLENCOURT. Inspected village with Town Major	Shm
do	2/3/17		To DENIER & BERLENCOURT re sundry matters. To ETREE WAMIN Re Arrangs for disinfection of billets. Inspected CAN ETTEMONT with Town Major. Interviews Town Major of REBREUVIETTE.	Shm
do	3/3/17		Inspected REBREUVIETTE with Town Major. Wate sanitary reports &sup	Shm
do	4/3/17		To trenches with Ashul. Work in WARLUS	Shm
do	5/3/17		To LIENCOURT. Inspected village with Town Major. Work in HAUTEVILLE	Shm
do	6/3/17		To WANQUETIN to 76th Bde re Thrush & anti-in disinfector. Inspected waggon lines of 40th Bde R.F.A. with m.o.	Shm
do	7/3/17		To ARRAS. Interviewed Sanitary Officer & inspected billets of 2/R.Scots, 1/R.Scots Fus., & 7/K.Shrop L.I.	Shm

Army Form C. 2118.

WAR DIARY of O.C. Sanitary Section
INTELLIGENCE SUMMARY

(Erase heading not required.)

Place	Date	Hour	Summary of Events and Information	Remarks and references to Appendices
WARLUS	8/3/17		To HAUTEVILLE. Arrange with No 5 Yard for use of Disinfector. Arrange with 76 F.Amb. for Disinfection of Blankets. Inspected billets in HAUTEVILLE. SMM	
do	9/3/17		To ARRAS with O.C. Sanser. 14F.D.W. to inspect sanitary arrangements & advance positions. To A.D.M.S. W.N.R. in WARLUS. He north out to ARRAS for sanitary work. SMM	
do	10/3/17		To MAGNICOURT. Inspected village with Town Major. To LIENCOURT, HAUTEVILLE & WANQUETIN. Water supply is doing. SMM	
do	14/3/17		To A.D.M.S., S.S.O., Camp Commandant, C.R.E. Arrange for supply of medical analyst for latrine construction in Adv. Dressing Station. Arranges with Sanser. for Disinfection of Blankets. SMM	
do	12/3/17		Wrote in WARLUS. To C.R.E. re supply of lunber. To WANQUETIN Inspected various sites. To No 7 Yard re disinfection of Blankets. To S.S.O. re coal supplies for disinfector. SMM	
do	13/3/17		To WANQUETIN. Inspected water supply & Pearsons, interviewed Town Major. SMM Report on wells in WANQUETIN (Hand) to Town Major. To HAUTEVILLE to No 8 Yard re disinfection of Blankets. SMM	

Army Form C. 2118.

WAR DIARY
or
INTELLIGENCE SUMMARY. of C.54 Sanitary Section
(Erase heading not required.)

Instructions regarding War Diaries and Intelligence Summaries are contained in F. S. Regs., Part II. and Staff Manual respectively. Title pages will be prepared in manuscript.

Place	Date	Hour	Summary of Events and Information	Remarks and references to Appendices
WARLUS	14/3/17		To HOUVIN HOUVIGNEUL. Interviewed area officer, arranged for relief of Nos 63 & 64 Stn. Sans. Sections there. Inspected MAGNICOURT. Interviewed Town Major. Inspected Sans. lys.-Bois. SMcM	
do	15/3/17		To WANQUETIN to 76th Bde re disinfector. SMcM To FREVENT, LIENCOURT, ETREE-WAMIN + BERLENCOURT with OC Baths re unkeep [sic] of baths, laundries. Inspected WANQUETIN baths + took any duties of OC baths. SMcM	
do	16/3/17		To LIENCOURT to advance store re underclothing supplies for baths. SMcM To WANQUETIN. To BERLENCOURT bath. SMcM	
do	17/3/17		To laundry at FREVENT. Interviews OC VI Corps Laundry re washing for 3D Division. To baths at BERLENCOURT, WANQUETIN + HAUTEVILLE. Paris 4000 francs re laundry infostafs [?] SMcM	
do	18/3/17		To ADMG General sanitary work in warlus. Conference at ADMG office re allotment of Sanitary Sections to areas. SMcM	
do	19/3/17		To FREVENT. Paid women at laundry. To MAGNICOURT. Interviews Town Major re latrines, Sanitary supply. Interviews Town Major at BERLENCOURT. SMcM To LIENCOURT to 76th Bde. to bath at HAUTEVILLE + WANQUETIN. Paid woman. SMcM	

WAR DIARY
or
INTELLIGENCE SUMMARY.

Army Form C. 2118.

F.O.C. 5th Sanitary Section

Place	Date	Hour	Summary of Events and Information	Remarks and references to Appendices
WARLUS	20/3/17		To ARRAS. Inspected cellars to be occupied by 9th Bde H.Q. To 9th Bde H.Q. Sanitary Officer ARRAS. Town Major Paw unable employed in laundry at AVESNES-LE-COMTE. SMW	
do	21/3/17		Paw women employed in washing at LE CAUROY. To ETREE WAMIN to Paymaster. To NOEUX vis Inspected Claufin Sulphur disinfector. To FREVENT laundry re supplies. To MANIN. C.R.Station repayment for washing. SMW	
do	22/3/17		To bath at HAUTEVILLE laundry at AVESNES. To WANQUETIN. Inspected camps of 4 Labour battalion with Camp commandant + advises as to drainage - latrine sites SMW	
do	23/3/17		To WANQUETIN to 8th Bde H.Q. that Paw women for washing. To Town Major WARLUS re increased sanitary fatigue to arrange I.S.O. re office SMW	
do	24/3/17		To ARRAS. Tested water of 3 wells near the bastion tooth sample. To 8th Bde H.Q. at WANQUETIN. To S.N.O. ADMS. Office. Town major WARLUS. SMW	
do	25/3/17		To baths at BERLENCOURT, HAUTEVILLE. To 76 Bde H.Q. at LIENCOURT. To S.N.O. ADMS re ham — To 8th Bde H.Q. at WANQUETIN. SMW	

Army Form C. 2118.

WAR DIARY
or
INTELLIGENCE SUMMARY
(Erase heading not required.)

O.C. SA Sanitary Section

Place	Date	Hour	Summary of Events and Information	Remarks and references to Appendices
WARLUS	26/3/17		Conference of STPOL with DADMS Sanitation 3rd Army. Individually more	
do	27/3/17		To FREVENT laundry. Paid women. To BERLENCOURT baths re clothing and supply. Also to Thayer re sanitation, village waste supply. To laundry at AVESNES. SHM	
do	28/3/17		To ARRAS. From OC No 9 Mobile Lab re testing fuels. To WANQUETIN to S Bde HQ. To MAGNICOURT - Interviewed Town Mayor. Sanitary insp in WARLUS SHM	
do	29/3/17		To ARRAS. Interviewed Sanitary Officer. To 3D Div laundry in ARRAS. To WANQUETIN. Baths & laundry at AVESNES SHM	
do	30/3/17		To WANQUETIN baths, SIBIBA HQ, Town Major. To HAUTEVILLE baths. Paid women at AVESNES. To TOURBÉCOURT. To FREVENT laundry. To JI Corps laundry SHM	
do	31/3/17		To ARRAS. Interviewed Sanitary Officer. To ADANG HQ, 1550 SHM	

B. Matthews
Capt RAMC
OC SA Sanitary Section

www.ingramcontent.com/pod-product-compliance
Lightning Source LLC
Chambersburg PA
CBHW081428160426
43193CB00013B/2221